Record of the Listener

Listener

Selected Stories from Hong Mai's *Yijian Zhi*

Record of the Listener

Selected Stories from Hong Mai's *Yijian Zhi*

Edited and Translated, with an Introduction, by

Cong Ellen Zhang

Hackett Publishing Company, Inc.
Indianapolis/Cambridge

21 20 19 18   1 2 3 4 5 6 7

For further information, please address
    Hackett Publishing Company, Inc.
    P.O. Box 44937
    Indianapolis, Indiana 46244-0937

    www.hackettpublishing.com

Cover design by Rick Todhunter
Interior design by Elizabeth L. Wilson
Composition by Aptara, Inc.

Library of Congress Cataloging-in-Publication Data

Names: Hong, Mai, 1123–1202, author. | Zhang, Cong Ellen, translator.
Title: Record of the listener : selected stories from Hong Mai's Yijian Zhi /
    edited and translated, with an introduction, by Cong Ellen Zhang.
Description: Indianapolis : Hackett Publishing Company, [2018] | Includes
    bibliographical references.
Identifiers: LCCN 2017039011 | ISBN 9781624666841 (pbk.) |
    ISBN 9781624666858 (cloth)
Classification: LCC PL2687.H887 A2 2018 | DDC 895.13/42—dc23
LC record available at https://lccn.loc.gov/2017039011

Contents

The 100 Stories

Acknowledgments

My fascination with supernatural tales began when I was a little girl. One of my most unforgettable childhood memories was listening to my grandmother and her friends tell fantastic stories about ghosts, gods and deities, and animal spirits. Imagine the surprise I felt years later when I realized that some of their stories might have come from the seventeenth-century anecdotal collection, *Strange Tales from the Liao Studio (Liaozhai zhiyi)* by Pu Songling (1640–1715). One of China's most famous storytellers, Pu came from a long line of enthusiastic recorders of "accounts of the strange and tales of the remarkable." This translation volume introduces another master in this genre, Hong Mai (1123–1202), who lived five centuries before Pu Songling.

Just like Pu's *Strange Tales*, Hong's *Record of the Listener* was decades in the making, but is also twice as long. The book represented an unabashed admission of the author's interest in the strange and the supernatural and provided rich material for our understanding of the everyday life in Song Dynasty (960–1279) China. After relying on Hong's work as primary source for multiple research projects, I began to incorporate some of his stories into my courses. The more *Record* material that I used, the more I found myself wishing that an English translation of selected stories was readily available. I am therefore extremely grateful to Valerie Hansen for recommending me to Rick Todhunter at Hackett Publishing when the press was considering a translation volume of the *Record*. Throughout the entire manuscript preparation and production process, Rick and his colleagues have been prompt in responding to my queries and meticulous in keeping track of the project's progress every step of the way. For their steadfast support, I am thankful.

Immense thanks are due to the two readers of the manuscript. Both went through my translation thoroughly, offering many general recommendations to streamline the text as well as numerous specific thoughts regarding style, the use of terms, and awkward or imprecise translations. I am also indebted to my dear friend, Kim Wishart, who edited the entire translation, making it much more readable. The book is far better as a result of their tremendous help.

The completion of the book is made possible by a publication grant from the East Asia Center at the University of Virginia. A Research Support in the Arts, Humanities, and Social Sciences grant at UVA paid for the map that appears in the Introduction.

My students in my Culture and Society in Imperial China seminar were the first to read the dozens of stories contained in this volume. I appreciate their questions about the text and the Song Dynasty, which pushed me to change some selections and helped shape the content of the Introduction. My son, Max, has remained an active participant in this project by listening to and going through the stories with me. I hope some of Hong Mai's fantastic stories will stay with them and many others in the years to come.

Introduction

Master Zhang, a resident of Lin'an (Hangzhou, Zhejiang), once went to a monastery and saw, in a ruined building, an ancient Buddha statue missing its hands and feet. Zhang brought the statue home, enshrined it, and worshipped it with devotion. Over a year later, the statue began to manifest its power. It would tell Zhang the family's fortunes and adversities in advance. This went on for twenty to thirty years.

During the Jianyan reign period (1127–1130), the Jurchens invaded Lin'an. Zhang fled in a hurry and sought protection in a dry well. In a trance, he saw the Buddha that he had been making offerings to coming to bid him farewell. The Buddha said, "Disaster will befall you, and you will die from it. I do not have a way to save you. The reason is that, in your previous life, you killed a man during the Huang Chao Rebellion (875–884).[1] The man's current name is Ding Xiaoda. He will get here tomorrow and kill you in revenge. Your life cannot be spared." Zhang was terrified [to learn about the approaching threat to his life].

Sure enough, the next day, someone holding a spear came to the well. The man shouted at Zhang and ordered him to come out. As soon as Zhang got out, the person attempted to kill him. Seeing that his death was near, Zhang called out, "Are you not Ding Xiaoda?" Astonished, the person asked Zhang, "How did

---

1. The Huang Chao Rebellion lasted from the mid-870s to the mid-880s and was one of the largest and most violent in Chinese history. Led by Huang, the rebels marched from north China to Guangzhou (in Guangdong) in the far south, slaughtering and pillaging along the way. They then turned back north, capturing the Tang capital cities Luoyang (in Henan) and Chang'an (Xi'an, Shaanxi), forcing the Tang emperor to flee. Huang then established the Qi Dynasty in Chang'an and declared himself the emperor. Tang troops seized Chang'an two years later. Huang retreated east, where he committed suicide a year later when most of his followers had been annihilated. The revolt tremendously weakened the power of the Tang court, which had been undermined by the An Lushan Rebellion (755–763) a century earlier.

you know my name?" Zhang then told Ding what the Buddha had said the previous day. Saddened by Zhang's words, Ding dropped his weapon on the ground and said, "One should resolve wrongs, not make enemies. In our previous lives, you killed me. If I kill you today, you shall kill me in later generations. When is this going to end? I now release you to get us out of this cycle. But if you stay here, you will surely be harmed by the horsemen coming behind me. You should travel with me for now."

Ding thus accompanied Zhang for several days. It was not until when he thought Zhang was safe did he send Zhang away. Ding was a native of Hebei who had been conscripted to serve in the Jin military.[2]

Entitled "Buddha Redresses an Old Injustice," this is one of over two thousand extant stories in the *Record of the Listener* (*Yijian zhi*, hereafter in text the *Record*) compiled by Hong Mai (1123–1202), an accomplished statesman, scholar, and writer in Southern Song (1127–1279) China. Given the *Record's* considerable size and the diversity of its topics, it would be impossible to select a single episode to represent an overarching theme of the collection. I have highlighted the above story for several reasons. First, it depicts an incident that took place in south China during the Southern Song, the *Record's* main geographical and temporal focal points. Second, the anecdote features another of Hong's main interests, two ordinary people: an urban resident and a soldier. Third, this particular story adds a human dimension to the traumatic events that characterized the Jin (1115–1234) invasion of the Song (960–1279), the fall of the Song capital Kaifeng (in Henan) and north China, and the violence that accompanied the Northern (960–1127) to Southern Song transition. As we will see shortly, this is a subject that resonated deeply with Hong Mai and his family. Finally, "Buddha Redresses an Old Injustice," like the majority of the tales in the *Record*, has at its center the religious ideas and practices of the general populace. More specifically, it reveals the strong belief in the efficacy of dreams and the penetrating influence of Buddhism in Chinese society. Upon encountering a badly damaged Buddha statue, Zhang did not leave it to further deterioration but instead

---

2. Hong Mai, *Yijian zhi* (hereafter *YJZ* in notes and source citations) (Beijing: Zhonghua shuju, 1981), *jia*:8.65.

brought it home and worshipped it with utmost dedication. Zhang's piety eventually brought the statue "back to life" and placed his family under Buddha's protection. Even more powerful is Hong's portrayal of the Buddhist notion of karmic retribution and Zhang's and Ding's understanding and transcendence of its meaning in response to Zhang's dream. Upon learning his crime against Ding in a previous life, Zhang was prepared to pay with his own, now that Ding had come to exact retribution. Even the Buddha made clear his powerlessness over the situation. Yet Ding, being a true follower of Buddhist doctrines, chose to end the vicious cycle. Not only did he forgive Zhang, he also ensured Zhang's safety from his fellow Jin soldiers. Hong Mai concluded his story without any further remarks on the consequences of Ding's merciful act. It might not be unreasonable to add, as Hong did in many similar stories, the following: that Zhang had been spared his life was a testament to his faithfulness to Buddhist teachings. Because of his compassion, Ding was rewarded with a long life or good fortune.

Even in the absence of such a narrative resolution, the tale is skillfully told and promises to provoke strong emotional responses in the reader, ranging from admiration and suspense to empathy and relief. Both ends of the emotional spectrum are vital elements of good stories and good storytelling. And a master storyteller Hong Mai was. Throughout the *Record*, Hong recounted, with an informal yet engaging voice, the deeds of omnipotent gods and vindictive spirits, filial and unfilial children, selfish and self-sacrificing parents, jealous spouses and shrewd servants, generous benefactors and cold-hearted avengers, wealthy merchants and humble peddlers, local hooligans and merciless bandits, and miraculous healers and effective prescriptions, all subjects of enduring public fascination. It would not be an exaggeration to say that anyone interested in the history, culture, and religious life of premodern China will find something to their liking in Hong's fantastic collection.

The one hundred stories included in this translation volume aim to provide students and the general English-language reader with a representative sample of Hong's work. The goal of this introduction is to provide some background for these anecdotes by outlining the history of the time in which Hong Mai lived, the Song Dynasty (960–1279), and Hong's life and career. This is followed by a brief overview of the *Record* as a work of miscellaneous writings (*biji*), the literary genre to which it belonged. The last segment of the introduction assesses the anecdotes presented in the *Record* as historical sources through a discussion of the work's content and themes.

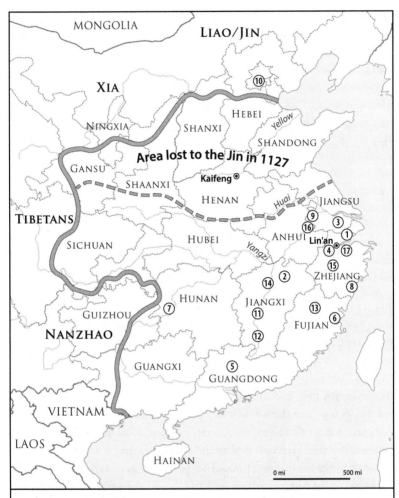

Song Dynasty and Important Places in Hong Mai's Life and Career

1 Xiuzhou *(Jiaxing, Zhejiang)*
2 Raozhou *(Poyang, Jiangxi)*
3 Wuxi *(in Jiangsu)*
4 Lin'an *(Hangzhou, Zhejiang)*
5 Yingzhou *(Yingde, Guangdong)*
6 Fuzhou *(in Fujian)*
7 Yuanzhou *(Huaihua, Hunan)*
8 Yongjia *(Wenzhou, Zhejiang)*
9 Jiankang *(Nanjing, Jiangsu)*

10 Yanshan *(Beijing, Hebei)*
11 Jizhou *(Ji'an, Jiangxi)*
12 Ganzhou *(in Jiangxi)*
13 Jianning *(Jian'ou, Fujian)*
14 Nanchang *(in Jiangxi)*
15 Wuzhou *(Jinhua, Zhejiang)*
16 Taipingzhou *(Dangtu, Anhui)*
17 Shaoxing *(in Zhejiang)*

Hong Mai's Time: The Song Dynasty (960–1279)

The Song dynasty was founded in 960 by Zhao Kuangyin (927–976, r. 960–976), a powerful military man at the court of the Zhou (951–960), the last of the five short-lived regimes that controlled north China following the end of the Tang Dynasty (618–907). In the next three decades, Zhao Kuangyin, posthumously known as Taizu, and his younger brother and successor, Zhao Guangyi (Taizong, 939–997, r. 976–997), consolidated their rule through the conquest of multiple regional states in different parts of the country, effectively ending the long-term political and administrative fragmentation that characterized the late Tang and the Period of the Five Dynasties and Ten Kingdoms (907–960).[3]

The Song Dynasty, which lasted for over three hundred years, has been conventionally divided into two large periods, the Northern (960–1127) and the Southern Song (1127–1279), based on the changes in the locations of its capital cities. During the first half of the dynasty, the capital was in Kaifeng in north central China. In 1127, the court moved south and eventually settled in Lin'an (Hangzhou, Zhejiang), where it lasted for another century and a half until its conquest by the Mongols at the end of 1270s.

The relocation of the Song court from north to south China was the result of a series of failed attempts by the Chinese state to deal with increasingly aggressive neighbors. In the eleventh century, these mainly included the Khitan Liao (916–1125) from the north and northeast and the Tangut Xia (1038–1227) from the northwest. To avoid prolonged and expensive campaigns, the Song signed peace treaties with Liao and Xia in 1005 and 1044, respectively, agreeing to make large annual payments in silk and silver. Both treaties remained subjects of heated political debates at the Song court, but they nonetheless assured a sustained peace along the Song-Liao and Song-Xia borders.

The rise of the Jurchens farther north broke the balance of this multi-state system. Following his unification of the Jurchen people, Aguda (1068–1123) of the Wanyan clan founded the Jin (1115–1234) in 1115 and quickly turned his attention to the Liao and Song. The collapse of the

---

3. For detailed introductions of the general history of the Song Dynasty, see Dieter Kuhn, *The Age of Confucian Rule: The Song Transformation of China* (Cambridge, MA: Belknap Press, 2009); and Peter Lorge, *The Reunification of China: Peace through War under the Song Dynasty* (Cambridge: Cambridge University Press, 2015).

Liao to Jin aggression in 1125 put the Jin and Song in direct confrontation. Kaifeng and the rest of north China fell to Jin attacks in 1127. In addition to ransacking the capital city, the Jin captured the last two Northern Song emperors, Huizong (1082–1135, r. 1100–1125) and his son Qinzong (1100–1156, r.1125–1127), the empress dowager, and thousands of court officials, royal family members, and palace women. The remaining Song court fled south and continued to fight the Jurchens under Zhao Gou (1107–1187), the recently enthroned Emperor Gaozong (r. 1127–1162), son of Huizong and brother of Qinzong. In 1030, Jin troops entered Hangzhou, the event that served as the backdrop for the story that opens this introduction. After repetitive setbacks in south China, the Jin finally agreed to a peace agreement with the Song in 1141. In addition to designating the Huai River as the border between the two states and the Song to be a vassal of the Jin, the treaty required the Song to pay large silk and silver subsidies to the Jin state.

Song-Jin relations, unlike Song-Liao and Song-Xia relations in the eleventh century, did not stabilize following the 1141 treaty. Military campaigns and diplomatic disputes continued to break out throughout the second half of the twelfth century. The Jurchens, however, were the first to feel the pressure of the rise of the Mongols, led by Genghis Khan (c. 1162–1227), in the early thirteenth century, and they fell to Mongol advances in 1234. The Southern Song held on by bolstering resistance along the Yangzi River, until its ultimate demise in 1279. For the next one hundred years, China was ruled by the Mongol Yuan Dynasty (1271–1368).

The violence accompanying the fall of the Northern Song and the founding of the Southern Song wreaked havoc in the lives of the rich and powerful and the ordinary Chinese alike, leading to sharp declines in population, large-scale dislocation and migration, and rampant banditry throughout north and south China. All of this can be readily observed in personal memoirs, literary works, local gazetteers, and official documents. Dealing with the Jin remained a central issue in Southern Song factional struggles. The rhetoric of the appeasement party, led by the all-powerful grand councilor Qin Gui (1090–1155), and those who favored a more aggressive policy in the hopes of reclaiming the lost territory, exerted a large influence on politics and intellectual life over the duration of the Southern Song, resulting in repressive government policies and systematic persecution and vilification of the opposing party by the dominant faction.

All the distresses and calamities aside, the Song Dynasty was the most advanced civilization of its time. China's population reached one hundred million around 1100, making it the most populous country in the world. For the first time in Chinese history, more people lived in the south than in the north, a trend that has continued for the last thousand years. This population may also have had the highest literacy rate in the world. By the twelfth century, every county and prefecture in the Song realm had a government school, with more advanced county school students being elevated to study in prefectural schools and the Imperial University in the capital.[4] It has been estimated that "In 1104, more than two hundred thousand students were on a government stipend."[5] The institutionalization of government education was complemented by the spread of private elementary schools and a growing number of academies.[6] An equally important contributing factor to literacy and evidence of its growth was the flourishing of the printing industry. In addition to enabling the wide transmission and preservation of official documents, literary and scholarly works, and religious scriptures, woodblock printing allowed for the mass production and circulation of many other types of materials, such as the *Record*, that were tailored to appeal to popular audiences.[7]

---

4. Throughout the Song, the number of counties fluctuated, ranging from "a low of 1373 to a high of 1495 in 1018–1019 during the Northern Song and from 875 in 1131 to 907 in the years 1223–26 and 1233 during the Southern Song." The number of prefectural-level administrative units similarly varied, reaching as high as three hundred in 1080 and as low as two hundred in 1208. Ruth Mostern, *"Dividing the Realm in Order to Govern": The Spatial Organization of the Song State (960–1276 CE)* (Cambridge, MA: Harvard University Asia Center, 2011), 48. The Imperial University (*Taixue*) was first established in the Han Dynasty (202 BCE–220 CE) and remained the highest government-sponsored educational institution in imperial China. Its size varied greatly throughout history, as did its structure and recruitment policies. In the Song, it enrolled between hundreds and thousands of students. Located in the capital city, the university provided students with major advantages in the civil service examinations and gave them political influence as well as access to scholarly opportunities.

5. Thomas H. C. Lee, *Government Education and Examinations in Sung China* (Hong Kong: Chinese University Press, 1985), 126–27.

6. See John W. Chaffee, *The Thorny Gates of Learning in Sung China: A Social History of Examinations* (Cambridge: Cambridge University Press, 1985); Lee, *Government Education and Examinations*; and Linda Walton, *Academies and Society in Southern Sung China* (Honolulu: University of Hawaii Press, 1999).

7. Lucille Chia, *Printing for Profit: The Commercial Publishers of Jianyang, Fujian (11th–17th Centuries)* (Cambridge, MA: Harvard University Asia Center, 2002); Susan Cherniack, "Book Culture and Textual Transmission in Sung China," *Harvard Journal of Asiatic Studies* 54, no. 1

The printing industry was also one of many areas that experienced major technological advances and changes in production. In the iron and steel industries, for example, the widespread use of coal in large workshops allowed China to produce 2.5 to 5 times as much iron in the Northern Song as England and Wales did in 1640.[8] In the shipbuilding industry, government-owned and private shipyards were capable of manufacturing a large variety of vessels, including warships, seagoing crafts, barges, passenger boats, ferries, and tow boats. "In 1021, the government ordered fifty-one shipbuilding centers to construct 2,915 barges specialized for the transport of rice, millet, and other grains," mainly from the southeast to other regions.[9] The large quantity of grains available to feed urban residents similarly attested to a significant increase in agricultural output. The main centers of rice cultivation in the lower Yangzi River Valley produced enough to satisfy the needs of the local population as well as the demand from the capital and other cities and towns. This, combined with improvements in the textile industry, raised the standard of living for a large portion of the population.

Agricultural productivity in turn facilitated the expansion of inter- and intraregional trade, making the Song one of the most commercialized and urbanized societies of its time. As the *Record* demonstrates, large urban and commercial centers could be found throughout the realm. The Northern Song capital, Kaifeng, had at least one million residents, creating a shortage of affordable living and working space. Compared to earlier times when commercial activities were restricted to certain parts of the city and residential wards were walled, Kaifeng's private residences and commercial establishments opened onto streets. The Southern Song capital, Hangzhou, was even more densely populated and saw a higher degree of specialization in commercial activities. Trade guilds, which first appeared in the Tang, numbered in the hundreds. Ordinary and wealthy people alike could find a large selection of goods and entertainments in the marketplace. The *Record* offers abundant evidence of similar developments in regional urban centers and townships. The trends in commercialization and urbanization were further

---

(June 1994): 5–125; Ronald Egan, "On the Circulation of Books during the Eleventh and Twelfth Centuries," *Chinese Literature: Essays, Articles, Reviews* 30 (December 2008): 9–17; and multiple articles in Lucille Chia and Hilde De Weerdt, eds., *Knowledge and Text Production in an Age of Print: China, 900–1400* (Leiden: Brill, 2011).

8. Robert Hartwell, "A Revolution in the Chinese Iron and Coal Industries during the Northern Sung, 960–1126 A.D.," *Journal of Asian Studies* 21, no. 2 (1962): 155.

9. Kuhn, *The Age of Confucian Rule*, 230.

facilitated by the emergence of a money-based economy and a currency system that comprised copper and iron coins, gold and silver, and paper money, a first in world history.[10] The number of coins (*qian*) in circulation in the Northern Song has been estimated at two hundred million strings (*min*), the equivalent of approximately 145 billion coins. Never again in the history of imperial China would the supply of coins reach such a scale.[11]

The Song government also distinguished itself from the earlier dynasties in the way it operated. Coming to power through a military coup, the founding emperors deliberately elevated the prestige of the civil service. By the early eleventh century, the central and local governments were run by a sophisticated bureaucracy. The appointment, evaluation, and relocation of government officials was determined through comprehensive personnel policies. Most important, compared to its predecessors, the Song recruited a much larger percentage of its bureaucrats through competitive civil service examinations. First installed in the late sixth century to counteract the influences of the great families and the military nobility, the examinations only allowed a limited number of successful candidates into officialdom in the Sui (581–617) and Tang dynasties. It was not until the Song that the system was significantly expanded and institutionalized. Held every three years on three levels, the examinations produced hundreds of degree-holders, the highest, and therefore most prestigious, being the *jinshi* (Presented Scholar).[12] The primary goal of the examinations was to select the most talented, knowledgeable, and conscientious individuals and bring them into government service. The testing assumed candidates' mastery of the Confucian classics, which placed high emphasis on moral cultivation and the building of a proper, hierarchical political and social order. Candidates

---

10. For a comprehensive discussion of the growth of the money economy, see Richard von Glahn, *Fountain of Fortune: Money and Monetary Policy in China, 1000–1700* (Berkeley: University of California Press, 1996).

11. *Qian*, or cash coin, was the most basic unit in the Song currency system. Designed as a round coin with a square hole, it was made of an alloy of copper and other metals. One thousand coins were threaded on a string, called a *min*. The number of coins in a string fluctuated greatly throughout the Song, usually falling somewhere between seven hundred and eight hundred, or even fewer, coins. Kuhn, *The Age of Confucian Rule*, 234. It should be noted that the number of coins may have reached a high point in the Song, but the use of silver bullion as a currency in the Ming and Qing periods meant that there was actually a much larger money supply in the late imperial times than during the Song.

12. The three levels were the Prefectural Examination, the Ministry of Ritual Examination, and the Palace Examination.

were expected to demonstrate their understanding of these principles when addressing questions regarding canonical texts, their abilities to draw on the classics in historical and political discussions, and their proficiency in applying key passages of particular texts to discourse on specific policies.

The Song examination system proved tremendously successful in attracting the brightest and most ambitious members of the social and educated elites to public service. While the number of degrees bestowed stayed relatively steady, the number of participants continued to grow, from tens of thousands in the eleventh century to hundreds of thousands a mere century later. In the thirteenth century, the passing ratio was as low as 1:400 in some prefectures in southeast China. The extreme competitiveness of the system, however, did not deter the most dedicated and socially conscientious from passing through the "thorny gates," as the examination halls came to be called. In fact, examination success and office holding remained the most desirable career path for China's educated and social elites until the early twentieth century, when the examinations were officially abolished.[13]

The appeal of the examination degree to Song educated men had much to do with the prestige of office holding and many other tangible benefits that were bestowed on officials and their families. These included the highest salaries of all previous and succeeding dynasties, tax exemptions, gifts and honorary titles for parents and even more remote ancestors, the privilege of protecting male relatives into officialdom (*yin*), and high standing in local societies.[14] More important, the examination system and the prominence of civil service created a new type of elite, the *shi* or *shidafu* (scholar-officials or literati). Lacking the pedigree of their aristocratic predecessors, Song literati distinguished themselves through a vigorous pursuit of examination success and political influence. But this group's prominence was also defined by its members' cultural and scholarly accomplishments: the Song produced some of the most celebrated poets, classicists, essayists, historians, and painters and calligraphers in Chinese history.[15]

---

13. Chaffee, *The Thorny Gates of Learning*.

14. The *yin* privilege allowed sons, grandsons, and other male members of high-ranking officials to enter government service based on these officials' merit, a measure that increasingly blocked social mobility in the Song period. For a systematic study of the failure of Song examinations in achieving fairness, see Chaffee, *The Thorny Gates of Learning*, 95–113.

15. For comprehensive surveys of major developments in Song literature and painting and calligraphy, see the chapters by Ronald Egan on the Northern Song and by Michael A. Fuller and Shuen-fu Lin on the Jin and the Southern Song, in Kang-i Sun Chang and Stephen

Another trademark of Song scholar-officials was their political activism. Deeply concerned with the threat to Chinese culture and identity from foreign invasions and alien influence, leading statesmen and intellectuals responded vigorously to what they perceived to be the critical issues of the day. These ranged from ineffective national defense and inadequacies in the education and recruitment systems to the state's role in managing the economy and the prevailing influences of Buddhism and Daoism in culture and society. Their enduring efforts to solve these and other problems are especially evident in the reform programs of Fan Zhongyan (989–1052) and Wang Anshi (1021–1086), which were responsible for fierce factionalism that outlived both the reformers and their programs.

Career setbacks and frequent changes in political atmosphere aside, both the reformers and their opponents fervently defended their positions in Confucian terms, a trend that can be clearly seen even in their discourses on factionalism.[16] This revival of Confucian rhetoric was not limited to the realms of education and politics. The Song was also one of the most intellectually exciting periods in Chinese history, culminating in the establishment of a "new" Confucian philosophy, the Learning of the Way (*Daoxue*) or the Learning of the Principle (*Lixue*). In an attempt to reestablish the centrality of the Confucian ideology and the superiority of their common cultural heritage, a line of Song thinkers, the most prominent among them the Cheng brothers of the Northern Song and the great synthesizer Zhu Xi (1130–1200) in the Southern Song, creatively appropriated classical Confucian thought, giving it new meanings, new structure, and a new textual basis.[17] Known in the West as Neo-Confucianism, Zhu Xi's ethical, social, and metaphysical philosophy went on to become the official curriculum of the civil service examinations in the Yuan Dynasty and onward and the ethical norms of the elite classes in China, Korea, and Japan. Through ritual manuals, family instructions, clan rules, and village covenants, Zhu's

---

Owen, eds., *The Cambridge History of Chinese Literature*, vol. I (Cambridge: Cambridge University Press, 2010), 381–464 and 465–556; and Wen C. Fong, *Beyond Representation: Chinese Painting and Calligraphy, 8th–14th Century* (New Haven, CT: Yale University Press, 1992).

16. Ari Daniel Levine, *Divided by a Common Language: Factional Conflict in Late Northern Song China* (Honolulu: University of Hawaii Press, 2008); and Peter Bol, *This Culture of Ours: Intellectual Transitions in T'ang and Sung China* (Stanford, CA: Stanford University Press, 1992).

17. "The Cheng brothers" refer to Cheng Hao (1032–1085) and Cheng Yi (1033–1107).

teachings were further instilled in the thoughts and everyday life of the general populace.[18]

Not all Song educated men were committed Neo-Confucians. Even those who were enjoyed diverse interests in their private and social lives. Song scholar-officials, for example, took pride in their large networks of friends, colleagues, and acquaintances, with whom they gathered frequently, drank profusely, told jokes, bantered, and exchanged marvelous stories. Additionally, the many long journeys these men took to participate in examinations and assume official posts brought them to diverse places, allowing them to gain access to sites of historical and cultural significance and accumulate knowledge about local natural conditions and social customs. These social and cultural activities were instrumental in transforming Song scholar-officials into great conversationalists and scholars of miscellaneous knowledge, and many sought to promote their credentials and expertise in these areas. The result was a rethinking of literati ideals and the emergence of a discourse on the importance of things "seen and heard" as legitimate, reliable historical sources. Hong Mai was among the most accomplished of this group of scholars.[19]

Hong Mai: Family, Life, and Career

Hong Mai was born to a well-known scholar-official family in Poyang of Raozhou (in Jiangxi). Not much is available about the family's ancestry. We

---

18. For several major studies, see Peter Bol, *Neo-Confucianism in History* (Cambridge, MA: Harvard University Press, 2010); Patricia Ebrey, *Confucianism and Family Rituals in Imperial China: A Social History of Writing about Rites* (Princeton, NJ: Princeton University Press, 1991); Patricia Ebrey, *Chu Hsi's "Family Rituals": A Twelfth-Century Chinese Manual for the Performance of Cappings, Weddings, Funerals, and Ancestral Rites* (Princeton, NJ: Princeton University Press, 1991); and Hoyt Tillman, *Confucian Discourse and Chu Hsi's Ascendancy* (Honolulu: University of Hawaii Press, 1992).

19. Cong Ellen Zhang, *Transformative Journeys: Travel and Culture in Song (960–1279) China* (Honolulu: University of Hawaii Press, 2011); "Of Revelers and Witty Conversationalists: Song (960–1279) *Biji* Writing and the Rise of a New Literati Ideal," *Chinese Historical Review* 23, no. 2 (2016): 130–46; "Things Heard in the Past, Material for Future Use: A Study of Song (960–1279) *biji* Prefaces," *East Asian Publishing and Society* 6, no. 1 (2016): 22–53; and "To Be 'Erudite in Miscellaneous Knowledge': A Study of Song (960–1279) *Biji* Writing," *Asia Major*, 3rd ser., 25, no. 2 (2012): 43–77.

do know that, by Hong Mai's time, the Hongs had lived in the region for over ten generations. Hong Mai's great-great-grandfather, Shiliang, moved to Poyang from Leping within the same prefecture in the early Northern Song. Shiliang's son died young. Shiliang subsequently took on the responsibility of educating his two grandsons, Yansheng and Yanxian, Hong Mai's grandfather. Yansheng became the first Hong man to receive the *jinshi* degree in 1085. The family's good fortune continued in the next generation when Hong Hao (1088–1155), Yanxian's son and Hong Mai's father, passed the examinations in 1115. Along with Hong Mai and his brothers, the three generations of Hong men not only firmly established their clan at the national level, they also helped elevate Poyang and Raozhou as places of culture and scholarship in the Southern Song.[20]

Hong Hao served in two local positions in the transitional years from the Northern to the Southern Song and gained the reputation as a caring and dedicated local administrator. According to his official biography, when a flood ruined the livelihood of the local people in Xiuzhou (Jiaxing, Zhejiang), Hong Hao proposed that the prefect use the rice that was being transported to the capital for relief. When his superior hesitated, Hong responded that he was willing to risk his life and career for the wellbeing of the Xiuzhou residents. Hong Hao's devotion to his subjects earned him the nickname, "Buddha Hong." Years later, this stellar reputation would spare his family from the looting and harassment of local bandits.

Hong Hao was sent on a peace mission to the Jin in 1129, two years after the Jurchens seized control of north China. This would turn out to be the defining event of his life and career. Hong's arrival coincided with the continuing advance of the Jin troops into south China. The Jin court had no intention of negotiating for peace with the Song at this time. Hong Hao was subsequently detained and banished by the Jin emperor to Lengshan (Nong'an, Jilin), where he remained for ten years and endured extreme hardships. He was

---

20. This brief introduction to Hong Mai and his life and career is based on multiple sources. These include several official biographies, including those of Hong Hao, Hong Mai, and Hong Mai's brothers, in *Songshi*, Hong Mai's *nianpu*, and works by modern scholars. See Tuo Tuo, *Songshi* (Beijing: Zhonghua shuju, 1977), 373.11557–74; Wang Deyi, "Hong Mai nianpu," in *Songshi yanjiu ji, di er ji* (Taipei: Guoli bianyiguan Zhonghua congshu bianshen weiyuanhui, 1964), 405–74; Chang Fu-jui, "Hong Hao, Hong Kua, and Hong Mai," in *Sung Biographies*, edited by Herbert Franke (Wiesbaden: Steiner, 1976), 464–78; and Alister Inglis, *Hong Mai's Record of the Listener and Its Song Dynasty Context* (Albany: State University of New York Press, 2006).

later transferred to the modern Beijing area. It was not until 1143 that Hong Hao was freed as a result of a large-scale amnesty by the Jin ruler.

Upon his return to the capital, Hong Hao was commended for his loyalty, personally received by Emperor Gaozong, and presented with generous gifts.[21] Hong's heroism and erudition promised to bring him much political influence. But disagreements with the all-powerful grand councilor, Qin Gui, and the hostilities between the two soon dimmed that prospect. Following a few brief local appointments, Hong Hao was exiled to Yingzhou (Yingde, Guangdong) in the far south, where he sojourned for eight years. He was eventually reinstated in 1155, but died on his way to the capital.

Hong Hao had eight sons, the most famous being the three eldest, Hong Kuo (1117–1184), Hong Zun (1120–1174), and Hong Mai. Often referred to as the "Three Hongs," Kuo, Zun, and Mai all passed the examinations in the 1140s, with Zun placing first and Kuo second in the 1142 palace examination. All went on to have successful scholarly and political careers. For a brief period in the mid-1160s, Hong Kuo even served as grand councilor. These accomplishments were especially outstanding in light of the fact that the three brothers came of age when their father's fate and even whereabouts were uncertain at best. In Hong Mai's case, Hong Hao's detention in the Jin meant that Mai did not have his father at his side from age seven to twenty-one. For this reason, the young Hong Kuo was praised for taking on the responsibility of supporting and protecting the family.

Hong Mai was born in 1123 in Xiuzhou, where Hong Hao was serving a junior position. Except for a brief period in 1130, during which the family returned to Poyang to flee Jin aggression, Hong Mai, his mother, Miss Shen (?–1138), and his brothers remained in Xiuzhou from 1123 to 1138. It was in Xiuzhou that the Hong brothers spent years studying and preparing for the examinations. It was also there that they witnessed the advancing Jin troops and the terror caused by the soldiers. When Miss Shen passed away in 1138, her body was returned to Wuxi (in Jiangsu), her native place, for burial, instead of being transported to the Hongs' ancestral graveyard in Poyang. Supported by their maternal uncle, the Hong brothers continued their study in Wuxi while in mourning. Unlike Hong Kuo and Hong Zun, Hong Mai failed the 1142 examination, but passed in the next round in 1145.

---

21. Emperor Gaozong went so far as comparing Hong to Su Wu (140–60 BCE), the famous Han Dynasty envoy to the Xiongnu, who was kept as a hostage for nineteen years.

In the decade after earning his examination degree, Hong Mai remained particularly close to his father while his brothers' careers accelerated. From 1145 to 1146, he lived in Poyang with Hong Hao, presumably while waiting for an official appointment. When Hong Hao was exiled to Yingzhou in 1147, Hong Mai accompanied his father on the long journey. It was only after Hong Hao had settled in Yingzhou that Hong Mai assumed a professorship in Fuzhou (in Fujian), where he stayed for over four years. As soon as he fulfilled his tenure in 1153, Hong Mai went to visit his father in Yingzhou. When Hong Hao died in 1155, Hong Mai took a mourning leave. Only after Hao's burial in late 1156 or early 1157 did Hong Mai leave Poyang for the capital.

Compared to many of his contemporaries, Hong Mai had a long service record. From 1145 when he passed the examination to his retirement in 1202, Hong occupied a great variety of official positions both in and beyond the capital, eventually reaching the ranks of Hanlin Academician and Vice Director of the Ministry of Personnel. Just like his father, Hong Mai was dispatched as an envoy on the occasion of a Jin emperor's enthronement. As soon as he crossed the border, disputes arose: in the official document that was presented to the Jin court, the Song emperor represented himself as an equal based on the terms of the 1161 treaty, instead of as the head of a tributary state, as specified in the 1141 peace agreement. Hong Mai was subsequently detained for three days before he succumbed to Jin pressure and acknowledged himself to be an official of a vassal state. Upon his return to Lin'an, he was widely criticized for having failed to live up to his father's example.

Despite this particular setback, Hong's career progressed smoothly. Among the positions that he held were imperial diarist, editor in the Palace Library, and drafter in the Secretariat and the Bureau of Military Affairs, which involved the preparation of numerous imperial edicts and pronouncements. Some of his most prominent official duties were completed while serving as a court historian in the Bureau of Compilation in the Historiography Institute. Altogether, Hong Mai participated in the compilation of the histories of the courts of four late Northern and early Southern Song emperors.

Hong Mai spent many years away from the capital in the 1170s and 1180s when he was appointed to Ganzhou (in Jiangxi), Jianning (Jian'ou, Fujian), Wuzhou (Jinhua, Zhejiang), and Shaoxing (in Zhejiang). In Ganzhou, he was said to have dedicated much energy to promoting education,

building bridges, and maintaining local order. The latter endeavor was especially effective: in several memorials, Hong reported that the prisons in Ganzhou were almost empty! As the prefect of Shaoxing, Hong took pains to
alleviate the heavy burdens imposed on local residents. More specifically, he
convinced the throne of the problems caused by the *hemai* policies.[22] His
advice led to more generous allowances, especially for the lower-grade households in the region.[23]

Aside from his government service record, Hong Mai's official biography and his contemporaries portrayed him as an outstanding scholar. He
was especially praised for his wide-ranging knowledge in the classics and
in earlier literary and historical works. In addition to serving as a court
historian, Hong wrote extensive commentaries on Sima Qian's (145–86
BCE) *Historical Record* (*Shiji*) and composed a history of the Southern
Dynasties (420–589).[24] Like his fellow scholar-officials, Hong composed
literary works for a variety of social occasions. These included funerary
biographies for family members and friends, *ji* accounts commemorating
the completion of landmark buildings, and poetic exchanges at informal
gatherings. His love for poetry can be especially seen in an anthology of
Tang poems that he compiled, which was said to have enjoyed wide circulation in the capital.

Above all, Hong stood out for his life-long interest in the investigation
of literary, historical, and institutional precedents and in recording stories
about ghosts and spirits. These efforts led to the compilation of two large
biji collections, *Casual Notes at Rong Studio* (*Rongzhai suibi*, hereafter *Casual Notes*)
and *Record of the Listener*. The following section turns to the *Record* in the context of *biji* writing in the Song.

---

22. According to common practice, the government issued loans in the spring to households
for them to turn in a certain amount of silk in summer and fall. Lower-grade households
were under the most pressure when they were required to pay this tax in currency, not in kind.
23. In the Song, rural households were categorized into five grades based on the value of their
property and the taxes they paid, including the village service duties. The top three grades
were called upper households, the fourth and fifth grades lower households. During the
Southern Song, the top four grades of households "bore far heavier service responsibilities
than the more numerous fifth-grade households." Brian E. McKnight, *Village and Bureaucracy in
Southern Sung China* (Chicago: University of Chicago Press, 1971), 127–29.
24. Hong Mai's dedication to historical writing is best illustrated by a personal undertaking:
he was said to have hand-copied the 294-chapter *Comprehensive Mirror to Aid in Government* (*Zizhi
tongjian*) by Sima Guang (1019–1086) three times!

Record of the Listener and Miscellaneous Writing in the Song

In the history of Chinese literature, the category *biji xiaoshuo* (miscellaneous writings and trivial anecdotes) referred to a large variety of works in classical Chinese. First appearing in the Period of Disunity (220–581), *biji xiaoshuo* gained importance in later times, with the Song being an especially high point of *biji* production. Whereas only dozens of *biji* have survived from the earlier periods, extant Song works number in the hundreds.[25] This development can be attributed to three major factors: the expansion of the publishing industry, the growing size of the scholar-official class, and the rising level of literacy among the Song population. Combined, these trends led to the wide circulation of printed materials in general, and the increase in *biji* authors and the demand for and popularity of anecdotal writing in particular.

Traditional scholars long struggled to properly categorize *biji xiaoshuo* in bibliographic terms and as a literary genre, not always agreeing that this was a genre at all. Modern scholars have continued to attempt a proper definition for *biji xiaoshuo* and to separate *biji* from *xiaoshuo*, which, in modern Chinese literature, designates the literary genre "the novel." So far, the most widely accepted working definition identifies three types of work as *biji*: (1) ones that mainly contain short stories, including "accounts of the strange and tales of the remarkable" (*zhiguai chuanqi*); (2) collections of anecdotal episodes on historical events and renowned historical figures; and (3) records of evidential investigation and authentication.[26] This classification, broad as it is, captures the wide-ranging and "miscellaneous" nature of *biji* writing: most *biji* works, including those by Hong Mai, are collections of short narratives on a large variety of topics. While some authors made conscious efforts to

---

25. The recently compiled *Quan Song biji* (*The Complete Song Biji*) (Zhengzhou: Daxiang chubanshe, 2003–2013) contains about five hundred *biji* collections. Scholars estimate that about three thousand *biji* works, in fragments or in their entirety, survived from the imperial times (221 BCE–1911 CE). *Song Yuan biji xiaoshuo daguan* (Shanghai: Shanghai guji chubanshe, 2001), preface.

26. Liu Yeqiu, *Lidai biji gaishu* (Beijing: Beijing chubanshe, 2003), 1–11. For an excellent introduction of the popularity of *biji* and the establishment of a *biji* tradition in the Song in English, see James M. Hargett, "Sketches," in *The Columbia History of Chinese Literature*, edited by Victor H. Mair (New York: Columbia University Press, 2001), 560–65. Also see Cong Ellen Zhang, "To Be 'Erudite in Miscellaneous Knowledge.'"

arrange their compilations in chronological or thematic order, most did not. In fact, it was a common practice among Song *biji* authors to state in the prefaces for their works that their *biji* were the result of years of casual record keeping of items gathered at social occasions or acquired through personal investigation. As a result, a typical *biji* would touch on various topics, ranging from observations about natural conditions to everyday life of the elite and ordinary people, and from local practices and customs to interesting person-alities and strange and unusual occurrences.

The miscellaneous nature of *biji* works can be observed in other ways. The sizes of *biji* collections, for example, varied greatly. Some contained only a few dozen short entries. Others included lengthier episodes and amounted to hundreds of chapters. Equally diverse were the backgrounds of *biji* authors. While towering scholarly and literary figures such as Ouyang Xiu (1007–1072), Sima Guang (1019–1086), and Lu You (1125–1210), composed *biji*, the majority of *biji* authors achieved neither high office nor literary fame. Their *biji* collections were often their only surviving works, bearing witness to these men's varied geographic and familial origins, travels, social connections, scholarly and artistic inclinations, and everyday concerns, such as personal hobbies, career aspirations, and obsessions.

As the author of two large collections, *Casual Notes at Rong Studio* and *Record of the Listener*, Hong Mai was, without a doubt, one of China's most accomplished *biji* writers.[27] Written and published in five installments over two decades beginning in 1180, *Casual Notes* includes twelve hundred entries in seventy-four chapters. The subject matters it covered are extraordinarily comprehensive. Hong Mai, for example, engaged in extensive study of the classics and the literary works of earlier scholars. He took it upon himself to identify and correct many errors regarding the evolution of government policies and institutions in the Song and pre-Song times. Also included in the *Casual Notes* was a large number of Tang and earlier verses, supplemented with Hong Mai's interpretations and his expression of admiration for the poets. Hong's other personal interests, such as divination, medicine, and the words and deeds of famous figures past and present, also found their way into the *Casual Notes*. The collection's various topics and its vivid narrative

---

27. The most comprehensive scholarly study of *Yijian zhi* in English has been undertaken by Alister Inglis. See Inglis, *Hong Mai's Record of the Listener*; "Hong Mai's Informants for the *Yijian zhi*," *Journal of Song-Yuan Studies* 32 (2002): 83–125; and Inglis, "A Textual History of Hong Mai's *Yijian zhi*," *T'oung Pao* 93, nos. 4–5 (2007): 283–368.

won it a large audience, including the Emperor Xiaozong (1127–1194, r. 1162–1189), immediately following its publication.

Even though both *Casual Notes* and the *Record* are classified as *biji* works, Hong Mai apparently meant for them to differ in their content and purpose. Compared to the *Casual Notes'* attention to the institutional, literary, and historical developments of the Song and earlier times, the majority of the *Record* stories were gathered through conversations and hearsay. If *Casual Notes* was more scholarly in nature and intended to demonstrate Hong's erudition in the classics, literature, and history and politics, the *Record* was a declaration of the author's love of the strange, the marvelous, and the supernatural, an interest that Hong professed in multiple prefaces to the different installments of the *Record*.

As a category of *biji xiaoshuo*, "Accounts of the Strange and Tales of the Remarkable (*zhiguai chuanqi*)" had a long tradition in Chinese literary history. From the Han onward, a large quantity of such accounts explored the delicate and complex relations between the living and the dead and the tensions inherent in the boundary crossings between the two realms.[28] The main concerns of the early authors—about the nature of the afterlife, the existence of ghosts, and the variety of human experiences in dealing with spirits and demons—were greatly expanded in the *Record*. Although he never categorized the *Record* as a work of *zhiguai*, Hong frequently marveled at the various types of strange occurrences that he had heard or observed and those that he had committed to writing. In this sense, Hong Mai was a master of accounts of the strange and the marvelous.

The *Record's* less scholarly background does not necessarily mean that Hong Mai considered his collection of stories as fictional in nature. In fact, Hong, just like his fellow *biji* writers, put substantial emphasis on the trustworthiness of his anecdotes. Throughout multiple prefaces and individual entries, Hong noted that all his stories were factually based on first- or second-hand sources and, in fact, should be treated as "unofficial histories." The title of the book, *Yijian zhi*, literally *The Record of Yijian*, followed a similar

---

28. Dirk Bodde, "Some Chinese Tales of the Supernatural," *Harvard Journal of Asiatic Studies* 6, nos. 3–4 (1942): 338–57; Robert Ford Campany, "Return-from-Death Narratives in Early Medieval China," *Journal of Chinese Religions* 18 (1990): 91–125; "Ghosts Matter: The Culture of Ghosts in Six Dynasties *Zhiguai*," *Chinese Literature: Essays, Articles, Reviews* 13 (December 1991): 15–34; and *To Live as Long as Heaven and Earth: A Translation and Study of Ge Hong's Traditions of Divine Transcendents* (Berkeley: University of California Press, 2002).

line of thought. Yijian was known as an extremely erudite person in ancient China. The Daoist classic, *The Book of Liezi*, states that "The Great Yü saw them (i.e., the large variety of marvelous things mentioned in the *Classic of Mountains and Seas*) in his travels, Boyi knew of them and named them, Yijian heard of them and recorded them."[29] By naming his book *The Record of Yijian*, Hong Mai implicitly compared himself to Yijian, the famous listener and recorder, and his *biji* collection to the *Classic of Mountains and Seas*.

In all likelihood, the *Record* was conceived in the 1140s after Hong Mai had spent substantial periods of time with his father upon Hong Hao's return from the Jin. Since Hong Hao kept a record of the things he had seen and heard in the northern state, which was published after his death, it was completely possible that his father's experiences inspired Hong Mai to prepare his own collection. Hong Mai might even have had a chance to go through his father's manuscript. In fact, some of Hong Hao's stories were included in the first chapter of the *Record*'s first installment, published in 1160.

The *Record* achieved an immediate success. In multiple prefaces, Hong Mai referred to its popularity and the pressure he was under to produce additional chapters in increasingly shorter intervals. In the next four decades, collecting remarkable and strange stories would remain one of Hong's major preoccupations. His amazing productivity had much to do with his diligence and the periods of semi-retirement in his official career. An equally important explanation for the long-term continuation of this project was the network of eager and dedicated informants that Hong Mai was able to maintain, and the *Record*'s reputation further enabled its expansion. In many prefaces, Hong readily acknowledged the contributions of family members, relatives, friends, and mere acquaintances, even including the names of his sources in many individual entries.

At the time of Hong Mai's death in 1202, the *Record* had grown to a massive collection of 420 chapters, totaling over four thousand entries.[30] Although it was not clear whether any complete editions were ever published by any Song publisher, we do know that multiple editions of varying sizes and qualities were made available by commercial publishing houses in different parts of the country. Much of the *Record* was nonetheless lost as early as

---

29. A. C. Graham, trans., *The Book of Lieh-tzu: A Classic of the Tao* (New York: Columbia University Press, 1990), 5.98.
30. The fourth series was not finished at the time of Hong Mai's death.

the Yuan Dynasty, an indication of the traumatic effects of the Song-Yuan transition. The current 207-chapter editions are based on post-Song redactions and extractions from Song and later manuscripts by traditional and modern scholars.

Understanding Song Culture and Society: *Record of the Listener* as Source Material

A large percentage of the *Record* stories, as can be seen when times and places are clearly marked in the text, occurred during Hong Mai's lifetime in the Southern Song, and feature the everyday lives of ordinary men and women in local societies. Any further characterizations of the *Record* would require an examination of a substantial sample of its anecdotes, an endeavor beyond the scope of this introduction. This section instead discusses the insights that the *Record* affords to our understanding of Song society and culture.

First and foremost, the *Record* stories are unique and valuable sources for the understanding of the religious ideas and experiences of both the educated elite and their illiterate and semi-literate counterparts.[31] They demonstrate, among other things, a profound belief in the existence of gods, ghosts, and animistic spirits and the rise of local cults and local deities. In fact, people in the Song believed that ghosts lived among humans; some were completely harmless, even benevolent, to the extent that female ghosts could develop genuine feelings for ordinary men. Still more sought to redress injustices or to repay debts from previous lives. Other tales depict a world in which Buddhist monasteries, Daoist shrines, or temples to the earth god, dragon kings, and nature gods and local deities could be found in the most desolate areas in the country, satisfying the needs of their followers in response to their devotional practices and routine requests. A large number of stories offer especially vivid details about the ritual services offered by the Daoist masters when they were invited to cure diseases, exorcize evil spirits, or perform divinations. Others are illustrative

---

31. For some major studies on religious beliefs and practices in the Song, see Edward L. Davis, *Society and the Supernatural in Song China* (Honolulu: University of Hawaii Press, 2001); Valerie Hansen, *Changing Gods in Medieval China, 1127–1276* (Princeton, NJ: Princeton University Press, 1990); and Robert Hymes, *Way and Byway: Taoism, Local Religion, and Models of Divinity in Sung and Modern China* (Berkeley: University of California Press, 2002).

of the influences that the Buddhist notions of birth and rebirth, salvation, karmic retribution, and transmigration of the soul had on the general populace, propagating in particular the certainty of retribution for good and bad deeds, and even good and bad intentions. Not surprisingly, the virtuous were compensated with official ranking, large fortunes, and long lives, while miscreants of all types, including murderers, thieves, bandits, cheaters, bullies, and unfilial children were severely punished by natural and supernatural powers alike. Many of these bad actors were taken to the underworld, where they witnessed gruesome scenes and received clearly reasoned judgments. Some suffered swift and ghastly deaths from lightning strikes or predatory animals. This belief in the close relationship between humans and natural and supernatural forces can also be seen in the widespread practice of geomancy, the belief in the efficacy of dreams, and the importance of recognizing and accepting one's fate. Numerous episodes in the *Record* convey the idea that one's life span, marriage, wealth, or fortunes in the examinations, often disclosed in a dream or by a fortune-teller, were predestined. This did not necessarily mean that humans considered themselves entirely powerless. In fact, Hong showed on many occasions that master geomancers and fortune-tellers could make adjustments to a person's fate. Similarly, individuals, by aligning their actions with the natural forces and by performing good deeds, could improve their lot.

Second, what makes the *Record* an invaluable source for studying the Song Dynasty is its extensive coverage of people from diverse class, professional, educational, and socioeconomic backgrounds. This effectively makes Hong's collection a guide to the social structures of Song local societies. At the highest level were low-ranking officials, students, and examination candidates. Along with the clerks and runners, these men were conspicuous for their education and their official and quasi-official status. A much larger component of Hong Mai's subjects were various property owners, whether members of landholding families, shopkeepers, hostel proprietors, traveling merchants, or peddlers of everyday necessities. Further down on the socioeconomic ladder were hired hands, who were mainly tenants, staff members at commercial establishments, and servants and maids working in rich households. Those who lived at the bottom and on the margins of society, including beggars, vagrants, robbers, and bandits, also receive a fair amount of attention in the *Record*.

Three additional groups of people merit special mention. The first, medical doctors, varied greatly in capabilities and credentials, as did the availability of their services. Hong's stories nonetheless show that, to well-off families, procuring medical assistance was a commonly accepted practice. The second group of people comprise men and women who handled the local populace's religious and ritual needs. In addition to those who were clearly identified as Buddhist and Daoist monks and nuns, this cluster included ritual masters, shamans, exorcists, fortune-tellers, burial specialists, and geomancers. The functions of these local "professionals" often overlapped with each other, and their reputations and experiences differed significantly, just as with doctors. The third group of individuals that deserve special attention is women. Compared to other Song authors of miscellaneous writings, Hong Mai gave far more attention to women. In addition to the aforementioned nuns, maids, and female exorcists, the *Record* includes episodes centered on courtesans, seductresses, midwives, matchmakers, and female entrepreneurs. The majority of women in Hong's stories, however, served in the traditional familial roles of daughters (-in-law), wives, mothers, concubines, and grandmothers.[32]

Third, in addition to giving insight on Song social structure, the *Record* exhibits, in concrete terms, the "connectedness" of the Song realm and the extent of its residents' mobility. The Song was held together by an extensive official road and waterway system.[33] Equipped with thousands of government-supported postal stations and lodging accommodations, as well as privately owned hostels and restaurants, this network allowed for timely communication between the political and administrative centers and the more remote and desolate regions. This same structure and its support facilities also made possible the movement of goods and people on a large scale. The *Record* brought this transportation system to life by depicting people from every corner of the empire moving across the country. Among the most frequent travelers were those on official business. This included students journeying to the capital or provincial centers to attend school or participate in

---

32. For comprehensive studies of the lives of Song women, see Patricia Ebrey, *The Inner Quarters: Marriage and the Lives of Chinese Women in the Sung Period* (Berkeley: University of California Press, 1993); and Man Xu, *Crossing the Gate: Everyday Lives of Women in Song Fujian (960–1279)* (Albany: State University of New York Press, 2016).

33. For general introductions of Song transportation and communication systems, see Peter J. Golas, *The Courier-Transport System of the Northern Sung*, Papers on China, vol. 20 (Cambridge, MA: East Asian Research Center, Harvard University, 1966); and Cong Ellen Zhang, *Transformative Journeys*, 43–68.

the examinations. Moving in the opposite direction, court officials and their entourage trekked long distances to assume local positions. Government couriers, both foot soldiers and messengers on horseback, rushed from one postal station to the next. An equally visible group of wayfarers were Buddhists and Daoists. On their way to visit temples and shrines, these monks and nuns came into direct contact with local residents. These encounters served as either backgrounds or main plotlines in some of Hong's most fantastic tales. The most conspicuous wayfarers in the *Record* were, without a doubt, merchants. That some maintained the same travel routes, and even stayed at the same inns year after year, reveals, more than anything, the ability of the transportation and communication system to connect disparate localities and regions and their economies. Understandably, women and ordinary farmers traveled in smaller spheres. But more than occasionally, we find them on the road looking for a doctor, attending religious services, visiting relatives, or joining festival celebrations in market towns.

Apparently, this infrastructure did not always run smoothly. The *Record* demonstrates in detail the inherent challenges of long-distance travel in the Song. Safety remained a grave concern. Natural disasters, such as shipwrecks and animal attacks, were responsible for many casualties along the way, as were malignant inn owners and rapacious bandits. Disorganization and inefficiency similarly created problems for travelers. The uneven distribution of inns, for example, often left travelers in limbo. The difficulties in maintaining correspondence between the people in transition and their families generated fear and anxiety on both sides. All these complications, while not surprising, provided the master storyteller Hong Mai with the ideal ingredients to describe the trials and tribulations of those who left behind the familiar for the unknown and the strange.

Fourth, other than shedding light on the material culture of travel and the personal experiences of the itinerants, the *Record* contains factual and anecdotal materials about the large changes in the Song economy, especially in regard to the ubiquity of contracts, commercial activities, and the impact of the monetary economy on daily life. Landholders of all sizes and their tenants remained the backbone of the rural economy. Hong's stories nonetheless show that the lines between landholding and commerce were rarely clear-cut as many families were involved in both farming and trade. In Hong's narratives, both villagers and townspeople had access to a market, where they could find the everyday necessities from pottery to cloth, and from cooking oil to foodstuffs such as meat, steamed buns, and roasted chicken. In addition to small peddlers, the most common establishments at the marketplace were wine and tea shops, restaurants, and hostels. Money, including copper and iron coins, silver, gold, and paper bills, was in wide circulation. Money lending and the use of contracts in sales and purchases of land and other commodities were commonplace. An especially interesting aspect of Hong's accounts is their many references to the great wealth that individuals and families possessed and the frequency with which this fortune seemed to change hands.

Fifth, while many of Hong's tales took place in bustling and fluid public places such as markets, inns, and wine shops, others occurred in the privacy of the domestic space. Collectively, they offer concrete evidence of the most significant values and ritual practices that were commonly upheld, even by those at the lowest echelons of society. These included ancestor worship, filial piety, betrothal and wedding practices, and a variety of death rituals. The *Record* is particularly illustrative of the tension and discrepancies between real-life scenarios and the ideals that were prescribed by government promulgations and found in didactic literature. Hong's depictions of the mundane aspects of everyday life as experienced by ordinary people can therefore supplement family instructions, village covenants, precepts for social life, and legal codes in deepening our understanding of Song culture and society. This can be illustrated through three examples: first, while caring parents and devoted children were depicted similarly in both standard didactic writings and in the *Record*, it is the latter that provides us with actual examples of selfish and irresponsible parents and ungrateful and negligent children; second, the behavior of chaste women and loyal servants is depicted rather uniformly across writings of different genres, but the *Record* offers abundant evidence of illicit affairs, premarital sexual relations, spousal betrayals, and cunning and manipulative domestic help; third, sibling rivalry, often exacerbated by partial or meddling parents, challenged normative ideas on family harmony and solidarity and proper hierarchies in the household.

Two more recurrent themes in the *Record* add to our knowledge about ordinary people's daily lives. The first is the centrality of property preservation and property disputes in family life. Many of Hong's stories feature individuals and families striving to increase the holdings of their estate, parents playing favoritism in property-related disagreements, brothers fighting for a larger share of the family assets, sons misappropriating their parents' belongings, or relatives and neighbors coveting each other's wealth. So often did conflicts, especially debt-related ones, arise that they necessitated the involvement of both the local government and gods and spirits. The other recurring theme in the *Record* is the emotional worlds of ordinary people. Hong Mai, for example, availed himself of a large vocabulary to describe his protagonists' fears and anxieties as they faced foreign invasion, local bandits, and final judgments from gods and spirits. He recorded with descriptive language the expression of genuine devotion between lovers and of children toward their parents and devotees to Heaven, the Buddha, and other gods and spirits. Also abundantly represented in the *Record* are the dreams of hopeful young girls thinking of their weddings and marriages, jealousy between spouses and hostilities between wives and concubines, the guilt felt by those who had committed evil deeds, and the terror of visiting the underworld or waiting for karmic retribution. Taken together, these stories allow us precious glimpses into the Song world, where men and women of all backgrounds went about their everyday routines, only to have them, more than occasionally, interrupted by unexpected changes in circumstance and encounters with something strange or marvelous.

Record of the Listener has been widely used by Chinese historians as source material in their scholarly works. In making selections for this volume, much effort has been made to avoid repeating the episodes that have already been fully or nearly fully translated by other scholars. This has in no way limited the scope of this volume, as many stories in the collection share similar themes.

The translations that follow are based on the most comprehensive and widely used edition published in 1981 by the Zhonghua shuju (Zhonghua Book Company).

Notes on the Translation

Citation

The volume, chapter, and page number of each story is provided at the end of the translation in parentheses. For example, (*YJZ, jia*:1.2), which appears at the end of the first translated story, means that the original story is found in chapter one, page two of the *jia* installment in *Yijian zhi* (Beijing: Zhonghua shuju, 1981). *Jia* ranks the first of the Ten Heavenly Stems, which Hong Mai used to name all the *Yijian zhi* installments. Other installment names that appear in this translation include *"yi," "bing," "ding," "zhijia," "zhiyi," "zhijing," "zhigeng," "sanzhi," "bu,"* and *"sanbu."*

Hong Mai's Informants

At the end of some of the entries, Hong Mai specified the person(s) from whom he heard the stories. His note shows in *italic* in the translation. For example: at the end of "Miss Chen's Ex-Husband (story number 5)," Hong added, *"Chen Yao (courtesy name Shiming) told this story. Chen was a good friend of Wu Sui."* At the end of story number 85, Hong recorded, *"Yu Weisi told this and the three previous stories."*

Official Titles

English translations for office and government agency titles generally follow those given in Charles O. Hucker, *A Dictionary of Official Titles in Imperial China* (Stanford, CA: Stanford University Press, 1985).

Romanization

I have adopted the *pinyin* system of phonetic transliteration for Chinese names throughout the book.

Place-Names

All place-names follow those given in *Zhongguo lishi da cidian, lishi dili juan* [Dictionary of Chinese history, volume on historical geography] (Shanghai: Shanghai cishu chubanshe, 1996). I keep all the original Song place-names in the text. Their modern equivalents are provided in brackets. When a place's Song name and modern name remain the same, I only provide the name of the modern province in which it is located. For example, "Luoyang [in Henan]" indicates that the name of Luoyang has remained the same and that it is located in modern Henan Province. When a place's Song and modern names are different, I provide both its modern name and the name of the province in which it is located. For example, "Lin'an [Hangzhou, Zhejiang]" means that the modern name for Song Lin'an is Hangzhou and that it is located in Zhejiang Province.

Local and Regional Administration

There were three levels of local and regional administration in the Song. The highest was Circuit (*lu*), followed by Prefecture (*zhou, fu,* or *jun*) and County (*xian*).

Chinese Names

In premodern as well as modern times, a Chinese person's surname or family name appears before his or her given name. For example, Hong was Hong Mai's family name and Mai his given name.

In addition to having a given name, most educated Song men acquired a *zi*, a literary, style, or courtesy name, as a symbol of adulthood and respect. One's *zi* was usually chosen by one's parents or teacher, but some individuals devised their own. *Zi* was used among friends, acquaintances, and people of the same generation or social status, while one's *ming* was reserved for the person himself and his seniors. Hong Mai had three commonly recognized *zi*: Jinglu, Yechu, and Rongzhai.

In the Song, illiterate or semi-literate men were often given a number as their first name, such as Du San (Three) in story number 25 and Chen Shisi (Fourteen) in story number 53.

Women did not usually have formal given names, but many had nicknames, such as Zhang Fo'er (Little Buddha Zhang) in story number 10 and Hua Buru (literally, flowers are not on par with her looks) in story number 98. Married women were most conventionally addressed as someone's wife.

I do not translate a person's name unless its meaning is relevant to the reader's understanding of the story.

Age

In traditional China, age was measured from the time of conception, not birth. Newborn babies were therefore considered as being one year old.

A Guide to Important Terms and Measurements

Date- and Time-Related Terms

Both for official purposes and in daily life, the Chinese mainly used the lunar calendar, which was based on the cycles of the moon's phases. The first day of the first month of the year in the lunar calendar usually falls between the second half of January and the first half of February in the Gregorian calendar. All the dates in this translation were lunar dates.

Geng (Two-Hour Period in Nighttime)

In traditional China, the nighttime, from dusk to dawn (about 7 p.m. to 5 a.m.), was roughly divided into five two-hour periods, called geng, which were announced by the beating of the drum. Whenever possible, I have converted the geng mentioned in the text into specific hours.

Nianhao (Reign Titles)

Starting from the Han Dynasty (202 BCE–220 CE), Chinese emperors employed one or multiple nianhao to number their reign periods. In addition to symbolizing imperial power, nianhao were also adopted to pray for good fortune, to convey imperial aspirations, and to mark the beginning of a new era. The majority of nianhao consisted of two characters.

Shi or Shichen (Two-Hour Time Period)

In traditional China, a day was divided into twelve two-hour periods, named after the twelve Earthly Branches. These periods were called shi or shichen. Whenever possible, I have converted the shichen mentioned in the text into specific hours.

Tiangan dizhi (Heavenly Stems and Earthly Branches)

From the earliest written records, the Chinese used the sexagenarian cycle to record days, months, and years. Each term in the cycle is composed of two characters. The first represents a character from a cycle of ten known as the *tiangan*, or Heavenly Stems, and the second from a cycle of twelve known as the *dizhi*, or Earthly Branches. A full cycle of pairings between these terms of ten and twelve generate a total of sixty different compound terms, a *jiazi*. Once complete, the cycle then repeats itself. The Chinese government officially adopted the Gregorian calendar in 1912. Whenever possible, I have translated *tiangan dizhi* combinations into specific years, months, or days.

Xun (A Ten-Day Period)

In traditional China, a month was divided into three *xun*, with one *xun* being ten days.

Currency-Related

Min or *guan* (A String or a String of Cash Coins)

A *min* indicated one thousand coins threaded on a string. The number of coins in a string fluctuated greatly throughout the Song, usually falling somewhere between seven hundred and eight hundred, or even fewer, coins.

Qian (Cash or Cash Coin)

Qian was the most basic unit in the Song currency system. Designed as a round coin with a square hole, it was made of an alloy of copper and other metals.

Measurements

Song dynasty linear, area, and weight and capacity measures mentioned in this translation are listed below. My main sources are James M. Hargett, *Treatises of the Supervisor and Guardian of the Cinnamon Sea: The Natural World and Material Culture of Twelfth-Century China* (Seattle: University of Washington Press, 2011); and Dieter Kuhn, *The Age of Confucian Rule: The Song Transformation of China* (Cambridge, MA: Belknap Press, 2009).

Linear Measures

1 *chi* = 10 *cun* = 31.6 cm or 12.6 in
1 *bu* = 5 *chi* = 158 cm or 6.3 ft
1 *li* = 360 *bu* = 568.9 m or 1,877.6 ft
1 *pi* (bolt of silk or cloth) = 4 *zhang* = 48 ft in length and 3.1 ft in width
1 *zhang* = 10 *chi* = 316.1 cm or 126.4 in or 12.0 ft

Area Measures

1 *mu* = 666m^2 or 0.16 acre

Currency

1 *min* or *guan* = 1 string of cash coins (*qian*) = 1,000 (often fewer) *qian* (cash coins)

Weight Measures

1 *jin* = 16 *liang* = 630 grams or 1.3 lbs
1 *liang* = 39 grams or 1.4 oz

The 100 Stories

1 • General Liu

Jiang Jing of Yixing [in Jiangsu] (courtesy name Shuming) was the magistrate of Anren in Raozhou [Poyang, Jiangxi]. The county had many perverse cults.[1] Jiang ordered all the statues there to be removed, demolished, and thrown into the river. He also banned the ordinary people from holding memorial services or offering sacrifices there. Altogether, Jiang had three hundred shrines eliminated. Because the Shrine for General Liu was considered the most efficacious, he did not want to abolish it, so the shrine was able to survive.

In the yard of the shrine there was a China fir tree. Its trunk and branches were massive and its shade extensive. Jiang planned to have the tree cut down. One day, as he napped in his zither studio, he dreamt of an extraordinary-looking person.[2] Arriving on horseback and in armor, the person stopped at the stairs and dismounted. Bowing deeply, he said, "My surname is Mumao.[3] I have resided here for a long time and have had the good fortune of receiving the Rector's kindness and protection.[4] I shall not dare to forget your benevolence. You will come back to this region in fifteen years."

Jiang woke up and realized that the man in the dream was a deity, but did not know what a Rector was. He nonetheless sighed with feeling and was amazed by the dream; Jiang subsequently left the tree alone and did not cut it down. In addition, he had the shrine's main hall and other buildings renovated.

When Jiang fulfilled his tenure, he went to the shrine to bid his farewell and left a poem on its wall that read:

> Although what I dreamt about was not real,
> The General quietly showed his power;
> The old shrine shined from now on,
> The ancient Chinese Juniper is green and luxuriant;
> Armor and horse I saw in the clouds,

---

1. In the Song, perverse cults referred to a variety of village medium-spirit cults that the court and local officials aimed to suppress in their effort to protect local society and regulate the everyday life of the common people.
2. The zither is a five- or seven-stringed musical instrument.
3. The characters "*mu*" and "*mao*," when juxtaposed, compose the character for Liu, the surname of the deity enshrined. By splitting the character into two parts, the deity seems to want to keep from exposing his true identity.
4. "Rector" is an official title. Here the deity hints at a future promotion for Jiang.

While lying and napping in the zither room;
I am leaving this poem not to record a strange tale,
In fifteen years, I will again knock on the shrine's door.

The stone on which the poem was inscribed still exists.

Fifteen years later, Jiang governed Shouchun [Shouxian, Anhui] and Jiangning [Nanjing, Jiangsu] at the rank of Secretariat Drafter, with Anren in the Jiangdong Circuit under his jurisdiction. His accomplishments qualified him for the bestowal of a new title at the Ministry of Personnel. When he returned to the court, he was given the title of Grand Rector. He died after having reached the rank of Auxiliary Academician at the Hall for Advancing Illustrious Administration. (*YJZ, jia*:1.2)

2 • The Daughter of the Shi Family

The Shis in the capital owned a teashop and used their young daughter to serve tea. Once there came a beggar, who suffered from a mental illness. He was filthy and his clothes were shabby. The beggar walked straight into the shop, asking for a drink of tea. The girl acted respectfully and brought him tea without taking any money. This recurred for over a month. Every morning, the girl would select fine tea and wait for the beggar. The father, angry at his daughter for not chasing the beggar away, whipped her, but the girl did not mind in the slightest. She provided for and waited on the beggar even more deferentially.

Several days later, the beggar returned and asked the girl, "Would you drink my leftover tea?" The girl was revolted that the tea was not clean and poured some on the ground. She immediately smelled an unusually fragrant aroma, so quickly drank what was left. Instantly, she felt that her mind was clear and her body strong. The beggar said, "I am Lüweng.[5] Although you

---

5. Lüweng literally means "Old Man Lü." Here it refers to the Daoist immortal Lü Dongbin, who legendarily lived in the Tang Dynasty (618–907) and was one of the famous "Eight Immortals."

did not have the luck to drink all my leftover tea, you can still obtain whatever you desire, be it wealth, official rank, or longevity."

The girl was from a modest family and did not recognize the importance of official rank. She only asked for a long life and inexhaustible wealth. After the beggar had left, she told her parents everything that had happened; shocked, the parents set out to look for the beggar, but he was nowhere to be seen.

When she reached pinning age [i.e., fifteen years old], the girl was married to a regiment commander. She later served as the wet nurse of the granddaughter of King Yan of Wu and was granted honorary titles for her service. The girl she nursed married Gao Zunyue and was given the title of Commandery Grand Mistress of the Kingdom of Kang. Miss Shi lived to the age of a hundred and twenty. (*YJZ, jia*:1.7–8)

3 • Prescription Given by Spirits

Huang Xi of Jianchang [Yongxiu, Jiangxi] said that a merchant from his home town once anchored his boat at Xunyang [Jiujiang, Jiangxi]. In the moonlight, the merchant saw dimly before him two persons conversing. One said, "Last night the offerings at Jinshan [Monastery at Zhenjiang in Jiangsu] were magnificent. I went to attend the ceremony, but the food and drink all smelled too bloody for me to approach. I was irritated that the cook had not taken greater care, so I dipped his hand in the cooking pot. It has since festered." The other person said, "The cook was surely at fault, but you have punished him too severely." The first person said, "By the time I regretted doing it, I could think of no way to rectify the situation." The other said, "How is this so difficult to fix? I have just the medicine to cure this—just grind some uncooked rhubarb into powder, then mix it with fine vinegar and apply the ointment to the sore. Not only does it alleviate the pain, it will also remove the scar. This prescription is most excellent. The only problem is that we have no way of notifying the cook [of the treatment]."

The merchant was just about to go to Jinshan. Having heard the conversation, he thought that, in the most incomprehensible way, this must have been the spirits' way of using him to inform the cook of this remedy. When he arrived at Jinshan, the merchant went to the temple to inquire about the incident. It turned out that there was a Retreat for Water and Land on the night when the two spirits visited.[6] When raising the cutting knife, the cook accidently hurt his finger, and blood dripped into the food. In a trance, the cook felt his hand being dragged into the pot by unknown forces. The resulting pain penetrated his bones; the cook could not stop howling and wanted to die instead. The merchant treated the cook according to what the spirits had instructed. The cook was cured in two days. (*YJZ, jia*:2.17–18)

4 • Cui Zuwu

Cui Zuwu was a native of Weisheng Commandary in Hedong Circuit [Taiyuan, Shanxi]. In the *guisi* year of the Zhenghe reign period [1113], he and my father were both living in the Tonglei Hall of the Imperial University. Cui said that he had been fond of women when he was young; not a day would pass without him consorting with a woman inappropriately. When he was twenty-six, he lay very ill and dying. There came a Daoist, Niu, who said to him, "If you could eliminate your sexual desires, I would save you." His parents [who were present] responded, "Our son is dying—if you could save his life, what would he not be willing to do?" The Daoist then gave Cui medicine and taught him breathing techniques, and ordered him to live in separate quarters from his wife; if he followed these instructions, his illness would be cured. It was three full years before Cui slept in the same room with his wife, but his sexual desires no longer arose.

---

6. The Retreat of Water and Land was a major Buddhist ritual that usually involved the summoning of the gods and the souls of the dead and Buddhist monks chanting the Diamond Sutra and other scriptures to pray for the salvation of the souls of all sentient beings, both in water and on land, from eternal suffering. The first such ritual was said to have taken place in the Jinshan Monastery at the beginning of the sixth century, held by Emperor Wu (464–549) of the Liang Dynasty (502–560), a devout Buddhist. This ceremony remained extremely popular in the Song.

Cui was thirty-five or thirty-six when he was studying at the Imperial University. His body was plump and he looked strong and handsome. He also got along well with people. If others took him to wicked places, he did not have to struggle to restrain himself because he simply did not have sexual thoughts. When drinking and eating, he would not get drunk or stuff himself. He said, "Excessive drinking and eating does the greatest harm to one's energy. It would take sixty days of cultivation to restore the body to its original state." Cui later returned to his native place. No one knows what happened to him. (*YJZ, jia*:2.19)

5 • Miss Chen's Ex-Husband

The daughter of Vice Director Chen Deying (courtesy name Tuo) was the wife of Shi of Kuaiji [in Zhejiang]. The couple had one son when Shi fell ill. Before he died, he held his wife's hands and bid her farewell, saying, "The love you and I have shared cannot be compared to that of ordinary couples. To repay my affections for you, take good care of my son. Do not remarry."

Miss Chen hesitated for a moment. Before she responded to the request, Shi became angry and said, "You wait on your new husband with care; do not think about your old master." He died after uttering these words. Miss Chen wept. Extremely saddened by Shi's passing, she became emaciated from longing for her husband.

Not long after Shi's death, Miss Chen's father was appointed to be in charge of Guangdong and took her with him. Pitying that his daughter was still in her prime, he chose a husband, Wu Sui of Putian [in Fujian], for her. Miss Chen declined the marriage without success. The family then accepted the bride price from the Wus.

Over a year after she was married to Wu, Miss Chen suddenly saw her ex-husband coming and cursing her, "You have treated me like this! How could you have married another man? I will take my son first and get you next." By dusk, their son died. Over a month later, Miss Chen too became ill and died. *Chen Yao (courtesy name Shiming) told this story. Chen was a good friend of Wu Sui. (YJZ, jia*:3.21)

6 • Duan Zai's Concubine

Duan Zai lived in a Buddhist monastery in Pujiang County in Wuzhou [Jinhua, Zhejiang]. Once his wife looked out at the entrance to the temple and saw a woman begging. The woman was in her prime. Duan's wife asked for the woman's name and background. The woman answered that she had neither a husband nor relatives through marriage. Duan's wife then said, "In that case, why did you not become someone's concubine, instead of begging for food? Would you be willing to come home with me?" The woman said, "It was not that I did not want to be a concubine; people were not willing to take me because I was poor and humble in origin. If I could take on the duty of serving your family, it would be a favor from Heaven."

Duan's wife then called the woman in. She had the woman take a bath and gave her clothes to change into. She then sent for the cook to teach the woman how to make drinks and meals. In ten days, the woman was capable of preparing everything. Duan's wife then had the woman trained in singing and playing musical instruments. In less than a month, the woman was extremely good at these as well. After receiving substantial guidance and training, the woman's looks also became quite impressive. Duan Zai named the woman Yingying and made her his concubine. This lasted for five to six years. Duan became so attached to Yingying that he worried that she might leave some day.

One evening, it was already past midnight. The Duans were all asleep. Someone from outside the gate called the doorkeeper and said, "I am Yingying's husband." The servant answered, "We've never heard that Yingying had a husband. Even if what you said were true, it would not be too late if you came in the morning. Why must you do this at midnight?" The person became rather irritated and responded, "If you do not open the door, I will come in through the cracks." The servant was furious. He went to knock on Duan Zai's door and informed Duan of the situation.

When Yingying heard about this, there seemed to be a joyful expression on her face. She said, "Here he comes!" and rushed out. Duan Zai worried that she might try to run away. So he lit a torch and chased her to the antechambers of the main hall. Duan only heard some loud sounds from inside the room before the lights went out. His wife sent maids to see what was happening. By the time the maids arrived, Duan was already dead, with blood streaming from his seven orifices [i.e., eyes, ears, nostrils, and mouth]. The lock on the entrance of the residence appeared undisturbed. The family never found out what strange beings Yingying and "her husband" were. *He Shuda of Pujiang told the story. I heard it from Cheng Zizhong. (YJZ, jia:3.22)*

7 • Jiang Bao's Deceased Mother

Once, while returning home at night, Jiang Bao, the servant of my fellow townsman, Ma Shujing, ran into a man dressed in white clothes. Together, they walked to the waterfront, where the man invited Jiang Bao to bathe with him. Jiang Bao was already undressed and about to get into the water when he heard someone calling his name. The voice seemed to come from far away. When it got closer, Bao realized that it was his dead mother's voice. His mother said loudly and quickly, "The man with you is not a good person. You must not bathe with him." In short order, his mother waded over and rushed to carry him back to the river bank. When they arrived at a residential house, she dropped Jiang Bao in the bamboo groves. People living in the house heard the noise and came out to see what had happened, but they saw only Jiang Bao; his mother and the white-clothed man were both gone. *Deng, Shujing's younger brother, told me this story. (YJZ, jia:4.31)*

8 • Merchant Fang Encounters a Robber

Fang of Wuyuan [in Jiangxi] was a salt merchant. While at Wuhu [in Anhui], he ran into a robber. The robber first tied up Fang's servant. He then cut open the servant's stomach with a knife and threw the servant in the river. The robber then turned to Fang. Fang prostrated in front of the robber, sobbing and begging for his life. The robber responded, "I already killed your servant, so I could not possibly spare you." Fang said, "I would like to say a word before I die." The robber asked what Fang had to say. Fang answered, "I have been devoted to burning incense ever since I was young. There are still several ounces of agallochum eaglewood in my traveling chest. Please allow me to open the chest and fetch it. I will burn the incense to express my gratitude to Heaven, Earth, and other deities. It would not be too late for me to die then." The bandit agreed to Fang's request.

The incense ran out a few hours later. The robber said, "Because I pity you, I am willing to spare you the knife." He simply bound Fang's hands and feet, weighed him down with a large rock, and threw him in the water.

At the time of his death, Fang had been away from home for several months. His family wondered why they had not heard from him. One day, Fang suddenly returned home. His wife scolded him, saying, "Why did you not send a messenger when you were on your way back?" Fang replied, "Do not be afraid of what I am about to tell you. I arrived at Wuhu on such-and-such day and was murdered by a robber. My body is currently at such-and-such place. The bandit's name is so-and-so and he is currently at such-and-such place. You must hurry and report this to the authorities." His wife, choked with tears, began to wail; Fang then disappeared. His wife subsequently informed the government office at Taipingzhou [Dangtu, Anhui] of the matter. The authorities captured the robber based on the information Fang had relayed to his wife. *Li Yong of the county told this and the previous stories.* (*YJZ, jia*:4:31–32)

9 • Cunning Clerks Commit Evil Deeds

The old petty official, Xia Hua, of Fuzhou [in Fujian], had been a clerk since the Zhiping reign period [1064–1067]. During the Zhenghe reign period [1111–1117], he was promoted to official rank due to his many years of service. From the time when he became a clerk to the end of his career, he served the local government for almost five decades. Xia once said that he had dealt with many prefectural officials and that everyone was deceived by people like him. The only two officials that could not be cheated were Cheng Gongbi (courtesy name Shimeng, c. 1030s–1080s) and Luo Choulao (courtesy name Ji, c. 1056–1124). Luo appeared very sharp at the beginning [of his tenure] and nobody dared to offend him. However, people later found ways to take advantage of him. Luo loved to learn; whenever he read a book, he would investigate its meaning. If he gained some insight, he would rejoice by making a long whistling sound. If he did not understand the book's meaning, he would scratch his head and loiter about. Clerks serving under Luo would wait to bring in official documents when he had just made long whistling sounds. Even if the documents contained fraudulent matters, Luo would not ask questions. But if the clerks approached Luo when he was scratching his head, even if the documents only included minor tricks or schemes, not a single one would escape his attention. Knowing Luo's habits, the clerks were able to deceive him. Hua said, "He loved to read books, yet was still deceived by us, how much more could we deceive those who do not?" *Zheng Dongqing of the prefecture told this and the previous two stories.* (*YJZ, jia*:6.52)

10 • Zhang Fo'er

In the tenth month of the second year of the Shaoxing reign period [1132], the Buddhist monk, Rizhi, of Xuanzhou [in Anhui] arrived at Xixiang in Huangyan County in Taizhou [in Zhejiang] and lodged at a mountain temple. The next day, the monks at the temple asked him to stay for a vegetarian meal before his departure. Two old villagers, Zhang and Chen, came to request that the abbot provide a service. Zhang said, "My fifteen-year-old granddaughter, Zhang Fo'er [literally, Zhang the Little Buddha], died suddenly last night. We were about to encoffin her early in the morning. Her grandmother, not bearing to part with her, hugged her while sobbing. My granddaughter opened her eyes all of a sudden and said, 'My entire body is wet. My hands and feet all ache.' We asked what had happened to her. She said, 'Two messengers came during the night. They chased me, tied me up, and escorted me across Cha Ridge, ten *li* [about five kilometers or over three miles] from Xixiang. I resisted, saying that I could not go with them, but was struck twice on the back with an iron hammer. It was extremely painful. There was a pond at the bottom of the ridge and a bridge over the pond. They ordered me to stand on the bridge, where I saw two people, folded in black quilts, being sent into a gate. The two messengers similarly attempted to wrap me in a patterned quilt, saying, 'You owe another family a thousand and five hundred cash coins. Now is the time to pay it back.' I implored with all my strength, saying, 'Allow me to go home and ask for money from my grandmother,' but they did not agree to my request. A person in green clothes next to us said, 'This girl heard an explanation of *prajna* before. She ought to be pardoned.'[7] The two messengers had no alternative but to throw me in the water and left. The water in the pond was very shallow. I was able to make my way to the bank and rush home.' I found the matter strange and amazing, so went to Cha Ridge to confirm it. Surely enough, I saw a pond right in front of the Chens' residence. So I called on the family head and asked, 'Who or what gave birth at your house yesterday?' Chen said, 'Our dog gave birth to three puppies. Two were black and one had spots. The spotted one was carried in the mouth by the mother and dropped in the water. It was already dead; only the two black pups are alive.' I told Chen what my granddaughter had said and offered him one thousand and five hundred cash coins. But Chen said, 'Your granddaughter never owed me money,' so was not willing to accept it. I thought to myself, 'If I do not repay this debt for my granddaughter, her life might not be spared in the future.' I therefore have come here with Old Chen."

The abbot subsequently provided a service for Zhang and Chen and gave the money to Rizhi. The abbot asked Zhang about the occasion that had afforded the granddaughter the opportunity to listen to an explanation of *prajna*. It was that she once went with her mother to the Hongfu Monastery in the county seat and heard Master Jingxiang lecturing on Buddha's teachings. (*YJZ, jia*:7.55–56)

---

7. In Buddhism, *prajna* refers to the insight into and knowledge of the truth of achieving enlightenment taught by the Buddha.

11 • Butcher Zhang's Father

In the eighth year of the Shaoxing reign period [1138], Butcher Zhang Xiao'er of Caoqiao in Pingjiang city [Suzhou, Jiangsu] went to purchase a dog from the Lius in Huangdi, fifteen *li* [about 7.5 kilometers or 5 miles] away from where he lived. Upon seeing Zhang, the dog wore a happy expression. It went straight to Zhang and embraced him. Zhang lifted the dog up by its ears to measure its weight and paid three thousand cash coins for it. The dog did not wait to be leashed and followed Zhang home.

Upon arriving at the Qi Gate, Zhang, afraid that the dog might run away, leashed it with a rope. The dog suddenly spoke in human language, "I am your father. I do not owe you money. You must not butcher me." Zhang, drunk and sleepy, did not understand the dog's words. He brought the dog home and asked his wife to prepare him a meal. The dog then said to Zhang's wife, "Come here, daughter-in-law. I am your father-in-law. I have not seen you and your husband for seven or eight years. Fortunately, I am now able to return home. I only owed the Lius three thousand cash coins and have now paid back the amount. You absolutely must not kill me. Your husband's life span is short. He only has one to two years to live. He should change his profession as soon as possible. Otherwise, he will not be reborn as a human in the next life. I am very hungry. You can bring me food now." The wife rushed to give half of Zhang Xiao'er's meal to the father-in-law without telling her husband. When Zhang asked for more after finishing his serving and was told that nothing was left, he became very angry. The wife said, "I gave half of the meal to father-in-law." She then told Zhang what the dog had revealed to her. Only then did Zhang become extremely frightened. The couple kept the dog and fed it, not daring to slaughter it. Three days later, the dog went to the Jiangs, where it bit people and was killed by the family. Butcher Zhang subsequently changed his profession and became a servant of an oil seller. (*YJZ, jia*:7.56)

12 • Luo Gong Condemned by the Underworld

Luo Gong was a native of Sha County in Nanjian [Nanping, Fujian] and studied in the Imperial University during the Daguan reign period [1107–1111]. There was a very powerful shrine in the University. Gong would silently pray for his future there day and night. One night, a spirit appeared in his dream and said, "You have already offended the underworld. You should go back to your hometown immediately. There is no need to ask about your future."

Because Luo Gong had rarely made mistakes in his personal conduct, he wished to be told the reasons for his offense. The spirit answered, "You do not have other faults. Your only mistake is that you have put off your parents' burial for a long time." Gong said, "I have brothers at home. Why has the blame been put on me alone?" The spirit replied, "Because you are a *ru* scholar who has learned about rituals and righteousness.[8] This is why you have been faulted for the wrongdoing. Your brothers are ordinary people, therefore unworthy to be held accountable."

Waking up from the dream and regretting his behavior, Gong packed up in a hurry and left for home. When fellow natives who lived in the same university hall inquired about his trip, Gong told them his dream. He died before reaching home. *Cao Ji told this story. Gong was the son-in-law of Cao's paternal grandfather's sister.* (*YJZ, jia:7.58*)

---

8. A *ru* generally referred to a scholar of Confucianism, which emphasizes the importance of virtuous behavior and ritual propriety. For failing to complete his parents' burial, Luo acted extremely unfilially. The next story conveys the same message to sons who were preoccupied with their scholarly and bureaucratic pursuits.

13 • Failing the Examination for Not Burying Father

Chen Gao (courtesy name Hengming) was a native of Fuzhou [in Fujian]. He arrived at the capital to participate in the Departmental Examinations after having passed at the prefectural level.[9] One day, he went to pray for a dream at the Shrine of the Two Gentlemen. That night, he had a dream in which a deity told him, "Your father has been dead, but you have not had him buried. Do not expect success in the examinations." Gao had his suspicions and did not believe in the accuracy of the dream. The next year, he surely failed the examinations at the Department of Ritual. Gao then sent a letter home, instructing his family to tend to the matter with urgency. He took the examinations for a second time and passed. *Li Shuchang of Ningde told this story.* (*YJZ, jia:*7.58)

14 • Son of the Lius

Liu Minqiu (courtesy name Haogu) lived on the outskirts of Kaifeng [in Henan]. His son became ill at two. Unable to bear seeing his son dying, Liu moved the boy to stay with the next-door neighbor, intending to wait for the son's death and then have him encoffined. One day, the wet nurse was holding the boy and sobbing when a Daoist master passed by. Taking a look at the boy, the Daoist said, "He is not dead yet." The master took out a pill and fed it to the boy, who then came back to life. He also asked for a piece of paper and wrote about ten characters on it, sealed the note, and handed it to the wet nurse. The master instructed that the note be carefully stored and not be opened and read. If it was read, the boy would die. The wet nurse secretly peeked at the note and was only able to recognize two numbers, "ten" and "nine." She did not know the rest of the characters.

---

9. In the Song, the examinations were held on three levels, the prefectural, the Department of Ritual, and the Palace.

From then on, the boy gradually recovered. His mother thought that he would not be spared when he turned nineteen.[10] When that year arrived, the mother ate a vegetarian diet and prayed to extend her son's life. Nothing happened to the boy. In the nineteenth year of the Shaoxing reign period [1149], Liu Minqiu served in a position in Jiankang [Nanjing, Jiangsu]. By that time, the son was already forty-three. He fell ill and died on the twenty-sixth day in the third month. His old wet nurse was still alive. It was not until then that the family opened the sealed note. They saw nine large characters written on it, which read, "The twenty-sixth day of the third month of the nineteenth year." *Liang Hongfu told the story.* (*YJZ, jia*:8.68)

15 • Unfilial Son Struck to Death

Wang Sanshi was a resident of the Xiaocheng Village at Poyang [in Jiangxi]. His parents originally purchased two coffins made of sandalwood in preparation for their deaths. Wang exchanged the coffins with two made of China fir from Xinzhou [Shangrao, Jiangxi]. He later sold those and replaced them with caskets cobbled together from Chinese ilex trunks. When Wang's mother died, Wang wanted to keep his mother's coffin for his own use, so he bought a pine coffin with which to bury her.

Ten days after the burial, Wang was struck to death by lightning. His body was left standing up on its side. Someone ran to inform Wang's son. Rushing to the site wailing, the son set his father's body flat on the ground. It was midday. Thunder rumbled and sent the son tumbling to a place about five *li* [about 2.5 kilometers or under 2 miles] away. By the time the son returned, his father's body was standing upside down. The son buried his father twice. Both times, the body was shaken out of the ground by thunder. Eventually, the son had a corner of his father's coffin cut off, covered the hole with bamboo, and buried the coffin. Everything remained quiet after that.[11] (*YJZ, jia*:8.71)

---

10. When combined, the characters for ten and nine could mean nineteen, nineteenth, or nineteen-year-old.

11. I have not been able to find an explanation for this practice. Presumably, it was intended to show that Wang Sanshi was interred in a broken coffin and did not receive a dignified burial since he failed to give his mother one.

16 • Doctors Wang and Li

Doctor Li, whose name has been forgotten, was a native of Fuzhou [Linchuan, Jiangxi] and a highly regarded physician. In ten years, his family's wealth grew to many tens of thousands of strings of cash coins. A wealthy man in Chongren County [in Jiangxi] fell ill and requested Li to cure him. The family promised Li five million cash coins as reward. Li went to treat the patient for about ten days, but the patient's condition did not improve. Li subsequently asked to leave so that the family could call on another doctor. He added, "You should not use just any other doctor. Only Doctor Wang is qualified."

At the time, Wang's and Li's reputations were of equal esteem. Both were excellent doctors. The patient's family agreed for Li to leave given that he had stayed for a long time and had not been able to cure the patient. Li then left some medicine with the patient and departed. Not halfway on his trip home, he ran into Doctor Wang. Wang asked where Li was going. Li told him what had just happened and that he had recommended Wang [to the patient's family]. Wang replied, "You were not able to cure the patient. My skills are far inferior to yours. It would be useless if I went. It might be better if we just went home together." Li said, "That would not be the appropriate way to deal with the situation. I got the patient's exact pulsation precisely and my prescriptions were equally proper. The reason I failed in curing the patient, in my view, was because my luck had run out. I was simply not destined to get the large reward. That was why I took my leave. You only need to go there. I will give you all the medicine that I have used. Treat the patient with it and he will surely recover."

Wang had always respected Li, so he followed Li's advice. When he saw the patient, all he used was Li's medicine. He only changed the decoctions slightly and had the patient alternate them. [Surely enough,] it only took three days for the treatment to take effect. The rich family was extremely pleased [with Wang's service] and sent him off with the reward, as had been promised.

Wang returned to the prefecture and prepared lavish gifts to offer to Li. Wang said, "I contributed nothing to the Chongren case. It was due to your instructions that I was able to cure the patient. I do not dare to keep all the reward money. I now present half of it as your birthday present." Li declined firmly and said, "I was not supposed to get the reward. That was why the patient did not recover under my care. It was all to your credit that he is well now. What contribution did I make? You cured the illness and I get the reward? This simply would not do." Wang could not force Li to accept the reward money. Another day, in the name of gift-giving, he purchased things that were worth thousands of strings of cash coins. Only then did Li finally accept them.

The two doctors were originally ordinary people, but were unyielding in their belief that righteousness was far more important than material gain. Even some scholar-officials might not be their equal. It has been several decades since the incident. People at Linchuan [in Jiangxi] are still fond of talking about their deeds. (*YJZ, jia*:9.73–74)

17 • Miss Tan's Moral Conduct

Wu Qi in the Qujiang Village in Zhenyang County of Yingzhou [Yingde, Guangdong] was somewhat educated and married to Miss Tan. In the second intercalary month of the fifth year of the Shaoxing reign period [1135], bandits arose around the county's Guanyin Mountain. They attacked and looted the village where the couple lived. Wu Qi was able to flee, but his wife and daughter were captured and, along with several women from the neighboring village, were forced to travel with the bandits. Among these women, Miss Tan's skin was clean and fair. A bandit subsequently wished to take her as his wife. Miss Tan despised him, saying, "You are a bandit. The official troops will come any time now. You will be completely wiped out. I am a woman from a good family. How could I possibly be willing to become your wife?" The bandit did not stop forcing his intentions on her, even to the extent of beating her. Miss Tan cursed even more, and eventually died from the bandit's brutality.

Later, when the bandits were eliminated, all the female captives from the neighboring village returned. They said, "If Scholar Wu's wife had not cursed the bandits, today she would be back too." The women went on to describe in great detail the way Miss Tan was murdered. Only then did Wu learn about his wife's deeds. Those who heard about her acts lauded her moral principles. I once wrote a biography for her. (*YJZ, jia*:10.84)

18 • Guanyin Cures an Arm[12]

An old village lady in Huzhou [in Zhejiang] had suffered from an arm ailment for a long time without being able to find a cure. One night, she dreamt of a white-robed woman calling on her and saying, "I suffer from the same condition. If you can cure my arm, I will cure yours." The old lady asked, "Where do you live?" The woman replied, "I am temporarily staying in the west wing of the Chongning Monastery." When the old lady woke up, she went to the Chongning Monastery in the city and told this dream to the monk Zhongdao in its west wing. Zhongdao thought about it and said, "It must have been Guanyin who appeared in your dream. There is a white-robed statue of her in my room. Her arm was accidently damaged during the renovation." Zhongdao then led the old lady to the room to admire and pay respect to Guanyin. One of her arms was, sure enough, damaged. The old lady subsequently hired laborers to have the sculpture repaired. As soon as Guanyin's arm was completed, the old lady's ailment was also cured. *Wu Jia of Huzhou told the story.* (*YJZ, jia*:10.88)

---

12. In Buddhism, bodhisattvas are enlightened beings who willingly delay entering paradise for the purpose of assisting others in reaching enlightenment. Guanyin, Avalokitesvara, is the most widely known and worshipped bodhisattva in China.

19 • Lin Ji's Hidden Merit

Lin Ji was a native of Nanjian [Nanping, Fujian]. When he was young, he once went to the capital. Arriving at Caizhou [Runan, Henan] on his way to the capital, he stopped at an inn for lodging. When he lay down to rest, he felt something on the bed pushing against his back. Lin lifted the mat and saw a cloth bag. Inside the cloth bag was a brocade bag. Inside the brocade bag there was yet another silk bag, which was stuffed with hundreds of northern pearls.[13]

The next day, Lin asked the inn owner, "Who stayed in my room the night before?" The owner replied that it was a rich merchant. Lin then told the owner, "He is an old friend of mine. If he happens to come again, please tell him to visit me at the Imperial University." Lin also left his name in the room, remarking, "On a certain day of a certain month in a certain year, Lin Ji of Jianpu lodged here." Lin then proceeded on his trip.

When the merchant arrived in the capital and went to fetch the pearls for sale, they were nowhere to be found. He rushed to look for them by retracing the route he had previously traveled. When he reached the inn in Caizhou and saw Lin's message, the merchant returned to the capital and called on Lin at the Imperial University. Lin told the merchant everything and said, "The pearls are all here, but you cannot simply take them from me. You may submit an official appeal at the prefectural government. I shall then return all the pearls to you there."

The merchant followed Lin's instruction. Lin went to the government office and handed all the pearls over to the merchant. The prefect ordered the merchant to divide all the pearls into two equal halves. The merchant said, "This has been what I wish to do." But Lin refused to accept the pearls, saying, "If I had wanted the pearls for myself, I would have seized them the other day." He ended up not taking anything. The merchant could not force Lin [to accept the award], so offered hundreds of thousands of cash coins

---

13. Northern pearls were found in bodies of fresh water in modern Jilin and Heilongjiang Provinces, which were under the control of the Liao (916–1125) and Jin (1115–1234). They were considered of higher quality when compared to the so-called southern pearls from Lingnan, a region which roughly corresponded to modern Guangdong, Guangxi, and Hainan Provinces. References to northern pearls can be traced back to the Han period (202 BCE–220 CE).

to provide a large ritual banquet at a Buddhist monastery to pray for good fortune for Lin.

Lin later passed the examinations and reached the rank of Grand Master of the Palace. He had a son, You (courtesy name Dexin). Dexin later served as a Vice Director at the Ministry of Personnel. (*YJZ, jia*:12.100)

20 • The County School at Liuhe

During the Jin conquest of the Northern Song [in the mid-1120s], all the buildings at the County School in Liuhe at Zhenzhou [Yizheng, Jiangsu] burned down completely. The students worked together to build a dozen or so thatched cottages as temporary living accommodations. Quite some time had passed before there was a discussion over moving the school to somewhere else.

There happened to be a temple in the county that had been deserted for years. When the bandits in the area ceased to wreak havoc, a monk began to beg money for its renovation. Once, when he was getting rocks in the outskirts, the monk got hold of two large boulders. Both were rather flat. The monk had the boulders moved over the ditches in front of the main hall of the temple. This way, the boulders were just like bridges.

The construction of the temple lasted for several years. It was nearly finished when the monk in charge of it died. Since he had no successor, the county government decided to turn the buildings into a school. Laborers were gathered to carry out the renovations and repairs. When the workers lifted the boulders for removal, they found two characters on the other sides of the boulders, "County School." No one knew when the characters had been inscribed there. That this temple was meant to be the county school seems to have been determined by fate. *Cui Yan (courtesy name Shuzhan) of the county told the story.* (*YJZ, jia*:12.104)

21 • The Qinghui Pavilion

Zhaozhou in Guangxi is a land of the worst kind of miasmic toxins, but its mountains and waters are quite delicate and graceful.[14] There was a pavilion named Tianhui [literally, painted by Heaven] in the prefectural garden. In the Jianyan reign period [1127–1130], the prefect Li Pi wished to change the name because it was a homonym of the reign title of the current emperor of the Jin state, [which had been threatening the Song court and just conquered the entire north China]. Li requested a new name for the pavilion from a former official, Xu Shichuan, but Xu did not come up with one for a long time. A man named Fan Zi eventually renamed the pavilion Qinghui [literally, clear brightness].

Xu visited Li when the plaque with the inscription of the new name had been installed and unveiled. After sitting in the pavilion for a while, the two, with walking sticks in hand, strolled around the building and saw a piece of stone in the dirt. The marks on the stone appeared to be written words, so Li ordered the stone taken out of the dirt and cleaned. The characters on the stone were actually the dedicatory record composed by Qiu Jun. Briefly, the record said, "I have selected a beautiful place and built this pavilion, naming it 'Tianhui,' because its surrounding scenery was so natural. In the future, on a certain day in a certain month of a certain year, a vulgar person will change its name to 'Qinghui.' This will call for a laugh."

When Li and Xu recalled the time when Fan Zi renamed the pavilion, there was not the slightest difference from what was indicated on the stone. (*YJZ, jia*:17.152)

---

14. In the Song, just as in the earlier times, Lingnan (literally, south of the Ridges), which included modern Guangdong, Guangxi, where Zhaozhou was located, and Hainan Provinces, was considered miasma-plagued, strange, and uncivilized.

22 • Yang Gongquan Dreams about His Father

Yang Gongquan (courtesy name Pu) was a native of Zizhou [Jianyang, Sichuan]. His father died in the *guisi* year in the Zhenghe reign period [1113], but had not been buried. The next spring, Yang dreamt about his father returning home and asked when he would pass the prefectural-level examination. His father said, "There was a recorder in the underworld, who was in charge of the registry for examinations. He was an old friend of mine. I once took the registry and went over it. Your name is not among those who earn the degree while the Three Hall System is in effect.[15] You will not realize your aspiration until the examination system is restored." The father then asked, "Gongquan, did you know that the court has implemented the Five Rites?"[16] Gongquan answered, "I did not." His father also asked about all sorts of family matters in great detail. When he finished talking, he left quickly, as if he was flying.

In the eighth month of that year, the court issued the New Five Rites, which stipulated that scholars who had not buried their parents were not allowed to enroll in school. Only then did Gongquan understand the meanings of his father's words. That winter, he managed his father's burial. In the *dingyou* year [1117], Yang Gongquan was promoted from the prefectural school to the Imperial University. Because he had been selected into the highest level of government school, Gongquan supposed that the dream, in which his father predicted his examination fortune, was not accurate. But nothing came out of his promotion. In the *xinchou* year of the Xuanhe reign period [1121], the Three Hall System was abolished and the examination system was restored. Yang passed the examination in the *jiachen* year [1124]. (*YJZ, jia*:18.157)

---

15. The Three Hall System was part of the reform programs that were implemented intermittently in the last decades of the Northern Song. It represented a departure from the long-established model of examination recruitment, in which candidates moved up from the prefectural level to the examinations at the Department of Ritual and the Imperial Palace in the capital. In the Three-Hall System, a unified, hierarchical school system served both the purpose of instructing students and selecting from among them the most capable to serve in the government. Each school on the county, prefectural, and imperial university levels was divided into three grades or halls, thus the origin of its name. The system was abolished in 1121.
16. The Five Rites referred to the ritual codes that were issued by the imperial government. The codes included five large components: sacrificial, death, military, guest, and weddings. All were highly hierarchical and regulated by the state.

23 • Flies at the Inn near Pucheng

A villager in Yongfeng, located in Pucheng [in Fujian], owned an inn. One day, a guest from Yanzhou [Jiande, Fujian], carrying a load of silk, rented a room to lodge. The guest stayed for several nights. The owner's wife was licentious by nature and seduced the guest to have sexual relations with her. She then told her husband, "The merchandise that this guest is carrying is large in quantity. Furthermore, he is traveling alone. We can plot against him." The husband therefore got the merchant drunk and, at midnight, tried to kill him with a knife.

The merchant called for help at the top of his lungs—his voice could be heard by the neighbors. [Unfortunately,] there were very few residents in the area. Only an old man from next door rushed to the inn. [Seeing the old man,] the wife quickly ran to stand at the door, blocking him from entering the inn with one hand while handing him a chunk of the merchant's silk with the other hand. The old man was pleased and left. The guest subsequently died.

Together, the husband and wife transported the merchant's body for burial in the saddle of a nearby mountain ridge about two hundred *bu* [about a quarter mile] away from the inn. Because the couple was in a hurry and terrified, the hole they dug was rather shallow. But there was no reason for them to suppose that their crime could be exposed.

Several months passed. The merchant's son wondered why his father had not returned from the long journey. Previously the son had accompanied his father on business trips and was completely familiar with all the roads that his father would travel and the inns at which his father would lodge. The son therefore took off to investigate and inquire his father's traces stop by stop. The merchant's tracks stopped at the inn. The son subsequently stayed there to look into the matter.

One day, he was sitting there in low spirits when a large fly landed on his arm. He chased the fly away but it came back. This repeated for several times. Since the son worried greatly about his father, he became very suspicious and prayed, "Might the spirits not have sent you to tell me something? If it is true, you can simply lead the way." [As soon as he stopped talking,] the fly suddenly took off, and the son followed it. The fly buzzed as if it were saying something and flew directly to where the merchant was buried. There were countless flies there. The son stuck out his head to look closely [at the pit] and saw that his father's body was right there.

The son ran to report the crime to the village militia, who arrested the murderers and delivered them to the county. The old man's wrongdoing was also exposed, and he provided clear proof of the crime. The inn-owning couple were both sentenced to death, and the old man was flogged in the back for acting as an accomplice. The government demolished the inn where the murder had occurred, and reduced the building to ruins. When Zheng Jingshi was on his way from Putian [in Fujian] to Lin'an [Hangzhou, Zhejiang], he passed by the place and saw that the houses had been destroyed and the murder scene had ceased to exist. This was the eleventh or twelfth year of the Chunxi reign period [1184 or 1185]. The merchant's injustice was redressed with the aid of a fly. This is similar to the story about the deer in Xinchang [Yifeng, Jiangxi]. The criminals in that story were caught and executed with the assistance of ghosts. (*YJZ, yi*:3.204–5)

24 • The Shrine for Court Gentleman Wang ✱
— maid turns into Wang and tells story

Wang Chun of Fuzhou (courtesy name Lianggong) served as the magistrate of Chong'an County in Jianzhou [Jian'an, Fujian] at the rank of Court Gentleman for Comprehensive Duty. One day, while performing his administrative duties, he quickly returned home without even finishing his steamed bun. Upon arrival, Wang fell to the ground and died. Two days after his death, Buddhist monks were chanting incantations in the hall when a young maid of the Wangs suddenly glared at the monks and chided them, saying, "You all get out. I have something to say in private." Her disposition and voice were no different from those of Wang Lianggong's.

The maid then sat down on the couch and sent a runner for the assistant magistrate, the recorder, and the sheriff. They all came, as did the clerk responsible for record keeping. The maid became furious, ordering the servants to seize the clerk and flog him one hundred times. The maid then told the county officials, "He is the one who murdered me. I had the strength to kill him [before I died]. But because of recent strange occurrences, I wanted to tell you what had happened: Several days before I died, I learned about a serious crime that the clerk had committed. So I chided him to his face and threatened, 'I will punish you to the firmest extent of the law.' He was angry and terrified, so he bribed the cook to slip poison into my food. The day before yesterday, I realized that I had been poisoned when I had eaten half of the steamed bun. I returned home in a panic, wanting to tell my wife and children, but died before I was able. Please open my coffin and see for yourselves. You will see if what I just told you is true."

Everyone, including the assistant magistrate, wept. Craftsmen were called in to open the coffin. Wang's entire body was rotten and oozing black liquid. The officials turned to question the clerk, who kowtowed and confessed. The clerk and the cook were both sent to the prefectural authorities. Because there was no suitable name for the crime that they had committed, the prefectural government did not want to execute them publicly, so had them secretly put to death in the prison. The county has now erected a shrine for Wang that is called the Shrine of Court Gentleman Wang. *Wang Jiasou told the story.* (*YJZ*, *yi*:3.210)

25 • The Unfilial Du San

There was a large well north of the Chongzhen Ward in Hongzhou [Nanchang, Jiangxi]. A resident, Du San, drew water from it to sell to residents. In the summer, he would sell mosquito medicine to support himself. He lived together with his mother and younger brother, who worked at a steamed bun shop, but Du San was the only one who supported his mother with two meals a day. However, Du was addicted to alcohol. If his mother acted slightly contrary to his wishes, he would humiliate, curse, and even flog her. Neighbors who witnessed his behavior would all sigh and wring their hands.

They even tried to convince the mother to sue Du. The mother had not been able to do so when, one day, Du came home drunk and beat his mother again. A short while after [he abused his mother], Du suddenly seemed to have gone mad. He took some of the arsenic and sulphur that he used to make mosquito poison, ran to the market, and asked for drinking water from people there. Those at the market thought that he had gotten drunk again, not knowing that the poison he had taken had begun to show its effects. Du died in an instant. Was this retribution due to his unfilial behavior? (*YJZ, yi*:7.242)

26 • Zhang the Cloth Merchant

Zhang, a rich old man in Xingzhou [Xingtai, Hebei], originally made a living through brokering small commodities and cloth. One evening, after the tea shop was closed, he heard someone outside the door, moaning and groaning with pain. He went out to see what was going on: the noise came from the convict that was flogged to death at the market during the day.[17] The convict said to Zhang, "I stopped breathing but have come back to life. I may be able to live if given some water. I fear that I would be put to death again were I to be spotted by the patrolling soldiers." Zhang therefore dragged the convict inside. Slowly untying the convict, he helped the man to a bed, providing him with a straw mat to sleep on. Zhang and his wife looked after the convict with care and fed him gruel and steamed bread. Even their son and daughter-in-law did not know about the matter.

Two months later, the convict's wounds had all healed and he could walk. Zhang gave him some travel money and personally saw him to the edge of town before dawn. He never even asked the convict's name or native place.

---

17. In traditional China, local and central governments routinely used the market as an execution ground.

As many as ten years passed. One day, a rich merchant, riding on a horse and being accompanied by servants, entered the market carrying five thousand bolts of cloth. Large agents contended to greet him. But the merchant asked, "Is Middleman Zhang here? I wish for him to sell the cloth for me." Everyone scoffed, then called Zhang for him.

Zhang declined the merchant's offer, saying, "My entire family's capital does not exceed several tens of thousands of cash coins. Yours is a large transaction. Please choose a wealthier and more senior person to help you." The merchant said, "It is my wish to impose this on you. You can simply find trustworthy shop owners, give them the merchandise on credit, and provide me with the contracts. I could go home and come back to collect the money later." Zhang did what the merchant instructed, but with hesitation.

After having stayed for several days, the merchant said to Zhang, "You can prepare some wine and have a drink with me; do not invite other guests." When the merchant arrived at Zhang's house, he asked Zhang's wife to join them. By the time he drank to his heart's content, the merchant got up and asked Zhang, "Do you recognize me? I was the man that you nurtured back to life at the bottom of your bed ten years ago. I had been a bandit my whole life. Going back and forth between a dozen or so prefectures, I had never failed until I came to Xingzhou. Here I was caught at my first attempt. Thanks to your kindness, I was given another life. As soon as I left the city gate, I swore to Heaven, 'From now on, I will never commit another murder. My only hope is to get a good amount of money to repay old man Zhang. I will steal no more either.' No sooner had I entered the Taihang Mountains, did I run into a person traveling alone. I robbed him and seized over a thousand strings of cash coins. I then became a merchant, buying and selling goods. I now have land and residences in Jin [Linfen, Shanxi] and Jiang [Xinjiang, Shanxi]. I am specifically using the cloth I brought to repay your and your wife's kindness. I am giving back to you the original contracts, so you can collect the money to build your estate. I will not return." He bowed, bid his farewell, and left.

The Zhangs subsequently became rich and the family's worth reached tens of thousands of strings of cash coins. People at Xingzhou call the family Zhang the Cloth Seller. *I heard this and the previous two stories from Jia Cinan.* (*YJZ, yi*:7.242–43)

27 • Old Woman Cui's Buddhist Hymn

The wet nurse of the Liangs at Dongping [in Shandong], old woman Cui, was a native of Zizhou [Qingzhou, Shandong] and the wet nurse of Liang Yuanming, Court Gentleman for Manifesting Rightness. Cui ate a vegetarian diet her whole life. Being extremely foolish, she was incapable of arguing right and wrong with her peers. Her mistress, Madam Chao, was devoted to Buddhism. Having stayed at Madam Chao's side day and night, all Cui could chant, however, was Amitabha.[18] Yet she was so dedicated that she never stopped chanting it. Since Cui did not use the rosary, there was no knowing how many tens of millions of times that she had recited the name.

In the eighteenth year of the Shaoxing reign period [1148], Cui was seventy-two and fell ill. She suffered from diarrhea and could not get out of bed, but her commitment to Buddhism and her chanting of Amitabha was even more sincere. Suddenly, nothing seemed to be wrong with Cui. She would frequently sing a hymn that said,

> On the way to the West [Paradise], it is easy to practice,
> There are no ridges above and no pits below;
> One needs not wear shoes and socks when one leaves for it,
> Wherever one steps, lotus flowers grow.

Cui would not stop chanting the hymn. People asked whose words they were. She said, "I composed them myself." They then asked, "When is the appointed time of your departure?" She answered, "During the *shen* hours [3 to 5 p.m.]." She indeed died during that time on the fifth day of the tenth month.

Cui was cremated in accordance with Buddhist customs. When the fire had died out, everything had been reduced to ashes but her tongue, and it looked just like a lotus flower. *Yuanming was my friend's son-in-law.* (*YJZ, yi*:9.262)

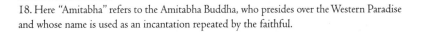
Cui became sick and sang to Amitabha and was healed, but then died

---

18. Here "Amitabha" refers to the Amitabha Buddha, who presides over the Western Paradise and whose name is used as an incantation repeated by the faithful.

28 • Royal Woman at Yuhang

In the fifth year of the Xuanhe reign period [1123], Tang Xindao was on his way from Kuaiji [Shaoxing, Zhejiang] to Qiantang [Hangzhou, Zhejiang] to participate in the examinations at the Fiscal Commissioner's office of the Liangzhe [Zhe East and Zhe West] Circuit and lodged at the Puji Monastery. In an empty room at the back of the temple, there was a coffin that had been temporarily left there. Tang wanted to see what was inside, but the monk at the temple stopped him, saying, "In it lies a woman. Her coffin is half-open, half-closed. She would come out often and associate with the living. It would not do unless several people went in together to see it." Tang responded, "How could a scholar be afraid of ghosts!" and went in by himself.

It was recorded on the coffin that the casket was that of a woman of the imperial clan. She held the honorific title of the lady of a certain county and had been dead for forty years. Inside the coffin was a woman in her twenties. The cosmetics on her face looked as if they had been newly applied. Her looks and colors were no different from those of the living. Tang marveled at it and came out.

Upon his return to Kuaiji, Tang described what he had witnessed to Wu Yu (courtesy name Cailao). Cailao said, "There is nothing extraordinary about this. When I sojourned at a temple at the Yuhang County [Hangzhou, Zhejiang], there was also a coffin for a woman of the imperial clan that was temporarily left in a monk's sleeping quarter. Every night, she would drink wine and sing and laugh with the monk. If there were no one else present, she also had sexual relations with the monk. When it turned light, she would return to the coffin, and the monk would escort her. This lasted for two years and gradually became known to the woman's father. The father was angry [to learn about his daughter's inappropriate behavior] and planned to move the coffin and burn the body. [As soon as the father made his intentions clear,] the woman's mother dreamt about her daughter. Sobbing sadly, the woman said, 'I unfortunately died young and was destined to have sexual relations with the monk. I know my salacious behavior has humiliated my parents. But I am already pregnant. If I do not get to give birth to this child, I will descend to hell and will be unable to escape from it for a long time. Please put off burning my body for three more months for me to fulfill this destiny. It would not make a large difference if you burned me after I gave birth.' The mother wept just as her daughter did and woke up. She then told her dream to the father, who became angrier and said, 'My daughter is dead and has been associating with a vulgar monk. Now she even wants to have his child. I cannot stand this humiliation.' He insisted on burning the body."

"That night, the mother and everyone in the family all dreamt about the woman visiting them and telling everyone the same things she had said to her mother earlier, only with even greater earnestness and anxiety, appealing to them several times. The next day, all pieced together what they had heard and informed the father. The father was a stubborn person; he only became more irritated. Without waiting for the chosen date to burn the coffin, he immediately called on people at the funeral home and provided them with firewood to start a fire. The hired hands cut the coffin into pieces with an axe and burned the body. The woman's belly was big. It broke off in short order. There was indeed a baby inside that already had form." *Xindao told the story.* (*YJZ, yi:*10.264–65)

★ Father killing dead daughter who is also pregnant for having relations w/monk while she is dead, but comes back @ night.

29 • Gong Gu Managing His Livelihood

Gong Gu of Fangcheng [Gu'an, Hebei] was a conniving person. His neighbor, the Zhous, had been wealthy, but suddenly, all the Zhou men died one by one. The only members that were spared were an old lady and her ten-year-old grandson. [Seeing an opportunity to take advantage of them,] Gong Gu prepared wine and invited the old lady over, tempting her with nice words. He helped the old lady understand her best interests by saying, "You and your grandson live alone and use your land, estate, and properties as protection. This is the same as opening the door to invite bandits in. Why do you not sell everything to me while you are strong and healthy? I will support you until the end of your life and raise your grandson until he reaches adulthood. What do you think?" The old lady was greatly pleased and put everything up for sale at a price that was not even two-tenths of the value of the estate.

As soon as Gong Gu took hold of everything, he chased the old lady and the grandson off the property and moved his entire family there. On the day of the move, he ordered several monks to prepare a Buddhist ceremony to celebrate the occasion and offer his gratitude. At midnight, loud noises came out of a well and echoed around the entire residence. The noises did not stop until dawn. Gong Gu nonetheless continued to live in the house.

A year later, despised Jurchens attacked Tangzhou [Tangxian, Hebei]. Dozens of the Gongs died. No one in the family was spared. (*YJZ, yi*:11.274)

30 • The Lius' Burial

The Junior Guardian Liu Yanqing was orphaned when he was young. He later lost his grandfather and divined to bury him in Bao'an Commandery [Zhida, Shaanxi]. Someone told him, "The mountain on which your family's graveyard has been selected through divination is very beautiful, but the pit itself is not of the best location. This was because the geomancer knew that choosing the best place for your family would be detrimental to him, so he kept silent and did not tell you. When it is time to open the ground, simply choose the spot on which the geomancer stands. Your family will be rich and powerful generation after generation."

Liu did what he was told [when the construction of the tomb began]. The geomancer, saddened and weeping with tears, asked, "Who told you to do this? This must be my destiny. There is nothing I can do! I will die less than a hundred days after the burial. If you promise to take good care of my family, I will repay you by selecting an auspicious day and time for the burial: You can move the coffins here on such-and-such day. Wait till you see a donkey riding a person. Then begin the burial ceremony. It does not matter what time when that happens." Hearing what the geomancer said, Liu became sad too, but doubted the geomancer's reference to a donkey riding a person.

On the day of the burial, the ceremony was put off till noon when the donkey of a villager, who lived at the bottom of the mountain, gave birth to a foal. The color of its fur was extraordinary. A fellow villager carried the foal on his back to show it to its owner. The Lius conducted the burial at that exact moment.

Three months later, the geomancer surely died. Yanqing's rank eventually reached that of Military Commissioner. His son Guangshi held the title of Grant Mentor and the Duke of the Region of Yang. *Liu Yaoren (courtesy name Shanpu) told the story. Shanpu was the son of Guangshi.* (*YJZ, yi*:11.275)

31 • Zhang Huizhong Informs the Tiger

Zhang Huizhong of Chengdu [in Sichuan], along with his sister's husband, Qiu, passed the circuit examinations in Sichuan in the twenty-sixth year of the Shaoxing reign period [1156], and traveled together to attend the palace examination. Before they got out of the Gorges, their boat wrecked in the river.[19] Qiu died in the accident; Zhang narrowly escaped with his life. After he was granted the examination degree, Zhang was appointed Recorder of Jingyan County [in Sichuan].

When he reached Xiazhou [Yichang, Hubei] on his trip home, Zhang received a letter from his family, informing him that his younger brother had died from an illness. Zhang grieved while rushing west. He rode a thin horse and had with him only one Sichuanese soldier to carry his luggage. After passing Wanzhou [in Sichuan], although it was approaching dusk, Zhang did not stop to spend the night and subsequently fell off a cliff. He was about ten *zhang* [120 feet] from the river bank. He had wounds all over his body, so could not get up.

A short while later, a tiger came. Leaping forward, the tiger held Zhang's hair bun in its mouth and was about to devour him. Extremely scared, Zhang hollered and said, "If you, Tiger, can understand, please listen to me. My mother is eighty. She gave birth to two sons and one daughter. Last year my brother-in-law drowned; this year, my younger brother died at home. I am

---

19. The Gorges here refer to the Three Gorges: Qutang, Wu, and Xiling, which are located between Chongqing and Yichang in modern Hubei Province on the Yangzi River. In Song times, this section of the river was considered the most dangerous of all water routes.

the only one who has survived and am going to support my mother with my modest official salary. If you eat me today, it is my destiny and there is nothing to be pitied. But what is going to happen to my mother?" As soon as Zhang started talking, the tiger released his hair bun. Lowering its head, it looked as if it were listening closely. When Zhang finished talking, the tiger left his side. But it circled around Zhang, as if trying to protect him.

After midnight, Zhang's pain stabilized. Sleeping on a rock, he dreamt of someone telling him, "It is almost dawn. You can take off now." When he woke up, it was already light. Climbing some low-hanging trees, Zhang scaled back up the mountain inch by inch. When he reached the river bank, the horse had not moved, but was still standing where it was. Zhang then got on the horse and proceeded with his journey. His official documents were all with him, but his luggage had been carried off by the soldier.

Zhang took on his official post. When he fulfilled his tenure, his mother died. Not long after that, Zhang also died. From these occurrences, it can be surmised that it was Zhang's filial thoughts that had saved him from his appointed death, which was forestalled solely for the sake of enabling Zhang to serve his mother. Animals know righteousness to such a degree! Compared to those who do not extend their hands when someone falls in a trap, instead jostle a rock against the person—these people are far inferior to animals. Can humans be not as good as tigers? (*YJZ, yi*:12.282–83)

32 • Son of the Zhangs of Longquan

The Zhangs, owner of a rice shop in Longquan County of Chuzhou [Lishui, Zhejiang], had a fifteen-year-old son. Once the son carried a basket of fresh fish to a stream to butcher them. Because the fish flapped nonstop, his knife accidently hurt his finger. It was extremely painful. Zhang laid down his knife to rest for a short while. Suddenly, he thought to himself, "I hurt a finger and it is so painful. Here the fish have been scraped of their scales and removed of their cheeks, with their bellies sliced open and tails cut off. The pain they have suffered can be imagined; it is just that fish cannot talk." Zhang therefore discarded all the fish into the stream and entered the deep mountains on the very same day, living in a stone cave and refraining from eating or drinking.

His parents wondered why their son did not come back home, thinking that he might have fallen in the water and drowned. It was not until the next Cold Food Festival that villagers who toured the mountain saw him.[20] His body looked like it was made of dried wax. He was hunchbacked and was so thin that his bones protruded, but his face was still recognizable. The villagers rushed to tell his parents, who wanted to bring Zhang home. But he turned his back without looking at them and said, "I am not a member of your family. Do not worry about me." His parents wept and went home.

Ten years later, Zhang's parents went to see him again. His skin and body had been restored to their former appearances, their colors pleasing and shining. People did not understand what had happened. He now has lived in the mountains for over twenty years. *Huang Dazhen told this and the previous three stories.* (*YJZ, yi*:12.289)

33 • Liu Ziwen

Liu Zong (courtesy name Ziwen) was the magistrate of Linjiang in Zhong-zhou [Zhongxian, Sichuan] in the early Shaoxing reign period [1131–1162]. After completing his tenure, he temporarily lived in the neighboring Dianji-ang County [Hechuan, Sichuan]. Ziwen had a six-year-old son, Shilao. One day, Ziwen suddenly saw a little boy at the side of his son's wet nurse. The boy was of similar height as Shilao. Liu thought that the wet nurse must

---

20. The Cold Food Festival usually falls on April 4 or 5, 105 days after the winter solstice. According to legend, the festival commemorated Jie Zitui (?–636 BCE), who, along with his mother, was burnt to death in Mount Mian (in Shanxi), where they had hidden, because Jie declined rewards from and refused to serve Duke Wen of the Jin, Chong'er (697–628 BCE), whom Jie served with loyalty and dedication when Chong'er was on a nineteen-year-long exile. Chong'er had meant to use the fire to force Jie out of the mountain. After the accident, Chong'er ordered that, every year on the day of Jie's death, people were not allowed to cook and could only eat cold food, hence the Cold Food Festival.

have had the boy from an adulterous relationship with a servant in the outer quarters.

Liu blamed his wife for this [illicit relationship]. His wife, Miss Li, was dull and weak minded and incapable of managing the household. But she knew that Liu's suspicion was false and answered, "There was no such thing." Ziwen became angry. At the time, he was already suffering from pain in his thighs and often used a walking stick made of a papaya tree branch, so he used the stick to hit his wife on the back and ordered her to get out. Ziwen then went to tell his mother his suspicion. His mother responded, "You must have misheard. How could you say something like this?" Ziwen sighed and was furious, saying, "Even my mother is like this. What hope is there?"

Returning to his living quarter, Liu tempted Shilao with snacks, asking, "With whom does your wet nurse sleep at night? Who is the little boy?" Shilao was astounded and could not answer the questions. Ziwen stepped forward abruptly and took hold of Shilao's hand, grabbing and dragging him nonstop. People nearby rushed to rescue Shilao, whose face was nonetheless hurt and bleeding.

Liu Ziwen then called the wet nurse in, wanting to chase her out of the house. He said, "It has been several years since you came to my home. My son has grown up, yet you ruin your reputation with illicit and scandalous behavior. For the sake of my son, I cannot bear to punish you. You had better go." The wet nurse wept and bowed out.

Ziwen watched her go. With a smile on his face, he said to the servants, "Her son has followed her out the door. Her disgraceful conduct has been exposed completely. But my family all wanted to cover it up for her. Why?" People knew that Ziwen was going to fall ill [due to his bizarre behavior]. Less than ten days later, he became sick and died. While sick, he said, "I argued with the prefect several times, but failed to convince him; it is not that you did not know. Why do you stay at my side and not leave?"

Later, Ziwen's younger brother, Zai, explained, "When Ziwen was an administrator for levied service in Kuizhou [Fengjie, Sichuan], there was a convict in the prison whose punishment could be either life or death. The prefect wanted to execute the criminal. Ziwen did not fight for the convict's life with utmost vigor, and the prisoner died in the end. What Ziwen saw while he was sick might have been that convict's ghost." *Ziwen was the older brother of my mother-in-law.* (*YJZ, yi*:13.290)

34 • Injustice to Concubine Ma

A Sichuanese woman, Miss Chang, first married Chu Chunqing of Yiyang in Tanzhou [Xiangtan, Hunan]. Because she and her husband's concubine, Ma, fought for Chu's favor, the two women became jealous of each other. Chang took advantage of Chu's leaving home and flogged Ma to death. Chu's official rank reached that of county magistrate before he died.

Chang remarried Cheng Xuan of Poyang [in Jiangxi]. In the second month of the second year of the Qiandao reign period [1166], she was about to give birth, but for three days, the baby did not emerge. In broad daylight, Chang saw Concubine Ma holding a stick and whipping her belly. Her husband Cheng Xuan called the Daoist monk, Xu Zhongshi, at the Tianqing Shrine to chant incantations to drive Ma away; the Daoist also gave Chang magic water. Chang then gave birth to a daughter, but became infertile afterwards.

The concubine's demon haunted Chang even more. Chang would cry out day and night, telling her husband that "The ghost uses the stick that caused her death to beat me. I cannot stand the pain, so told the concubine that 'I did not intend to kill you. It was the maid who used the stick excessively that accidently took your life.' But the ghost said, 'It was all your idea. What else do you have to say?'"

Cheng again asked the Daoist monk to come to the house; this time the Daoist sent a Heavenly general to chase and catch the ghost. The ghost told the general, "I died from extreme injustice. Although the Master is respectable, what could he do to me since justice is on my side?" People all saw Miss Chang in bed, arguing very hard with someone. The Daoist did not think he could succeed in bringing the ghost for punishment. He therefore tried to enlighten her with kind words and promised to chant abundant scriptures and incantations to assist her in the underworld. The ghost nodded her head and left.

Five days later, the ghost came back again and said, "The power of the scriptures and incantations can only help with my rebirth. But one who murders should pay with her life. Surely Chang is not to be spared." [Hearing this,] Chang said, "In that case, I will die for sure. Although I regret what I did, it is too late for me to do anything. When the concubine died, she left behind hairpins, earrings, and clothes that are worth hundreds of strings of cash coins. They ought to be given back to her now, in case these things will cause disasters in my other lives." Chang then called the ghost over and asked, "Would you want copper coins or spirit money for your belongings?" The ghost laughed and said, "I am a ghost, not a human. What would be the use of copper coins?" The family then purchased a hundred batches of spirit money and burned them while chanting prayers. When the smoke died out, so did Chang. It was the sixth day of the third month. (*YJZ*, *yi*:15.311–12)

35 • Xu Si Suffering from Forgetfulness

Xu Si (courtesy name Yansi) was a native of Yongkang in Wuzhou [Jinhua, Zhejiang] and held in high esteem by his neighbors and people in the prefecture for the quality of his literary work. Villagers who wanted to erect [commemorative] steles and inscriptions for their ancestors would go to ask him. Throughout his entire life, Xu never stopped reading books for a single moment. He later returned home after serving as the controller-general of Jianzhou [Nanping, Fujian].

In his old age, Xu suddenly suffered from forgetfulness and could not tell apart the myriad things in the world. When meeting guests and friends face to face, he would not recognize them, even to the extent that he treated his wife and children as strangers when they were right in front of him. When he ate meat, he did not know that it was meat that he was consuming. When he drank wine, he did not know that it was wine that he was swallowing. He acted the same with hunger and thirst, cold and warmth, and changes in day and night. He could not write even one character. This lasted for three years before he died. This might have happened because Xu had studied so hard and thought so painstakingly that he had lost his mental faculties. *Yu Liangneng told this story.* (*YJZ*, *yi*:15.315–16)

36 • The Daughter-in-Law of the Wangs of Yunxi

In the fall of the seventh year of the Zhenghe reign period [1117], the daughter-in-law of the Wangs at Yunxi in Wuyuan [Wuyuan, Jiangxi] died, but came back to life a day later. Zhu Qiaonian (courtesy name Song) of the same county was reading books by the creek at the time. [When hearing this,] he rushed to the Wangs and asked what the daughter-in-law had seen. The woman said, "As soon as I entered the room from outside yesterday, I saw two clerks waiting outside the door. They then took me off with them, walking in the desert. It was dark; I could not tell whether it was morning or dusk. In a short while, we entered a large city. The market and the city were very prosperous. All our relatives and neighbors who had died earlier were there. They were shocked to see me and asked why I had come. The clerks who chased me there led me into a government office. We passed by the west wing and stood solemnly in a room, where a clerk looked up the register and pointed at my name, asking, 'Are you the daughter of the Yus of Wuyuan in Shezhou [Shexian, Anhui]?' I answered, 'Correct.' He continued, 'Are your father's and grandfather's names so-and-so and the name of your village so-and-so?' I said, 'Those are incorrect.' The clerk was embarrassed and said, 'There has been a mistake.' He chided those who took me there and ordered them to go find the right person. A long time later, the clerks came back holding another woman. Her body and flesh were dripping wet. Several babies circled around her, pulling and dragging the front and back of her clothes. The clerk asked the woman's surname, ancestry, and place of origin. All the information she gave matched with what was recorded in the register. He then ordered that she be put in prison. Turning to me, the clerk said, 'She has the same family name as you, so you were accidently caught and led here. Altogether, that woman killed five sons. Her sons appealed their injustice extremely urgently. Although her life span was not used up, the underworld authority had no other alternative but to register her early. When you return to the living world, you should tell what you have seen to people in the world. Be sure not to kill one's children recklessly.' He then ordered someone to see me out of his office. The person pushed me into the river. I then came back to life." Qiaonian, along with people in Miss Wang's family, went to inquire after the family of the chased woman. She had surely died on that day. *Qiaonian wrote an account to record this incident.* (*YJZ, yi*:16.317–18)

37 • The Reincarnation of Wang Xin

Wang Xin (courtesy name Hengzhi) was a native of Jiangyin [in Jiangsu]. He passed the examination in the *wuchen* year of the Shaoxing reign period [1148]. While waiting to fill a vacancy as Professor at Yangzhou, he died at home in the third month of the *yihai* year [1155] before he could assume the position.

That winter in the tenth month, a tenant of the Wangs saw a man riding a horse, with two soldiers handling the animal. When he looked closely, he realized that it was the professor. In shock, the tenant asked where Wang was going. Wang answered, "I am going to Scholar Yin Qian'er's at Pengsong." The tenant said, "Pengsong is more than ten *li* [about five kilometers or over three miles] away from here. It is already dusk. I am afraid that you might not be able to get there in time." Xin said, "Distance is not what I worry about. It would help if you could lead the way for me." The tenant then accompanied Xin.

A few hours later, they arrived at the Yins' door. Wang Xin got off the horse and handed the servant a paper bag, saying, "Thank you for coming with me." He then suddenly entered the house through a crack in the door.

The servant was extremely scared. He hurried home and looked at what was inside the bag. There were fifty copper coins. He did not dare to tell people what had happened. The next day, he went to inquire. It turned out that the Yins' granddaughter-in-law had given birth to a son that night. *Yan Kangchao told this story.* (*YJZ, yi*:17.326.)

38 • Young Woman of Shuzhou

Su Yanzhi of Pengzhou [Pengxian, Sichuan] served as the administrative supervisor in Shuzhou [Chongqing, Sichuan]. He had a daughter who was about eight or nine years old. One day, the girl played at the corner of the bed and saw a small hole in the ground that was lit-up. She probed it with a tube, but the tube fell into the hole. The girl ran to tell her father, who measured the hole with a long pole. The hole was so deep that the pole was not long enough to reach its bottom. When Su took the pole out, he saw decayed brown silk attached to it. Su thought it extremely strange, so called in laborers to break the ground. After digging for about ten feet, they found a dried-up body, complete with its head and feet. He had the body encoffined and buried in the open country.

The next day, there was suddenly a good-looking woman moving around in the room. When people in the family cornered her and asked who she was, she went to hide in the wall cracks. In the end, they did not get to question her. At the time, a scholar in the prefecture, Chen Yu, had just come from Langzhong [in Sichuan]. Chen was good at practicing physiognomy and was capable of fending off ghosts and demons using Daoist techniques. Su therefore called Chen to examine the matter.

In a short while, a woman came and said, "I was the daughter of the Duans in Hanzhou [Guanghan, Sichuan] and was engaged to the Tangs in the same prefecture. When I was about to be married, the Tangs unexpectedly broke the original contract because my family had suddenly become poor. Since I did not get to marry anyone else, I was sold to be the concubine of the Recorder Fei in this prefecture. Unfortunately, I was favored by the master due to my good looks and was buried alive by the mistress. It has been several years since that happened. If it had not been for Master Su who had me reburied, I would have been a roaming ghost. It's just that when I was first dug out, the laborers were not careful and almost broke my shin bone. Presently, I cannot walk, so have no alternative but to stay here. I have no other intentions." Chen said, "What is difficult if you want to leave? I will arrange it for you." He took a piece of paper and cut it into the shape of a person and said, "He can be used to carry you." The woman smiled, thanked Chen, and left. That night, Yanzhi's older sister-in-law dreamt about a servant carrying this woman, who bowed twice and bid her farewell. *Huang Zhongbing told this and the above stories. (YJZ, yi:20.360–61)*

39 • Daughter of the Wens

In the fourth month of the third year of the Qiandao reign period [1167], a daughter of the Wens in Yongzhou [in Hunan] reached her pinning age [i.e., fifteen years old] and was engaged. Two nights before her wedding, she dreamt about a person dressed in yellow leading her to the government office. The judge there, in a green robe and wearing a scarf, greeted her and said, "You are needed here because there was a mistake regarding some official business, which has led to a large lawsuit that has gone on for fifteen to sixteen years. It has involved many people. You go home for now [since it is not your turn yet]. Come back tomorrow." The girl woke up and told her parents the dream, but neither had any idea what the judge meant.

The next night, the girl again dreamt about arriving at the large hall. A kingly person sat at the desk and the judge presented him with the official documents [involving the girl's case]. The king decreed, "Correct this [mistake]." Immediately, someone brought a cup of decoction to the court for her to drink. It was extremely smelly and disgusting. The girl woke up as soon as she was out of the door. By then she had turned into a man.

Her parents were shocked and sent a messenger to inform the son-in-law. The in-law's family thought that Wen was not a woman in the first place and that Wen's parents had intended to swindle them. They subsequently brought a lawsuit at the prefectural government. Only after an investigation uncovered the truth was the lawsuit dismissed. Wen's voice and bearing did not differ from when she was a woman; the only difference was that (s)he had changed into men's clothes. It was said that the in-law's family once again wished to marry Wen to their daughter and make Wen their son-in-law. (*YJZ, bing*:1.370–71)

40 • Fei Daoshu

Fei Shu (courtesy name Daoshu) was a native of Guangdu [in Sichuan]. In the *gengzi* year of the Xuanhe reign period [1120], he was on his way to the capital. When he approached Chang'an [Xi'an, Shaanxi], he stayed at a lodge next to the Yanzhi Slope. By the time Fei put down his luggage, the sun was already setting behind the mountains. The daughter-in-law of the lodge owner, leaning against the door, smiled at him and inquired with concern about the hardships on the road.

In the middle of the night, the woman came to Fei's room alone and said, "I secretly admire your honor's elegant demeanor and would like to offer you pleasure for a moment. Would you allow me?" Shocked, Fei asked, "Who are you? How did you end up here?" The woman answered, "My father is a silk trader in the capital. My family lives in so-and-so ward. My family married me to the son of the hostel owner. My husband is already dead, but I am too poor to return to my family. Unable to stand sleeping alone, I approached you at the risk of shaming myself." Fei said, "I would not want to violate you. Now that I truly understand your situation, I will go to find your father and ask him to send for you. Please do not resent me." The woman was embarrassed and left unhappily.

Fei arrived at the capital. One day, he passed by the very ward and found the silk merchant's residence. He announced his name at the entrance and expressed the wish to meet the master of the house. The master asked, "Who is the caller? And how did you have any association with me?" Fei answered, "I am Fei Shu from Shu [i.e., Sichuan]. Earlier when I passed by Chang'an, I ran into your daughter. She had entrusted me with something. Therefore, I have come to visit you." The old man rushed to receive Fei and said, "I had a dream one night, in which a spirit told me that my daughter was about to lose her chastity to someone. If she had not encountered you, she would have been in real danger. Your name matches exactly the one in my dream. I would like to hear what you have to say." Fei told the old man about his encounter with the old man's daughter; with tears running, the old man bowed to thank Fei and said, "The spirit said that you would be a high official. That ought not to be presumptuous talk."

After leaving the old man's house, Fei calculated and realized that the old man had the dream at the exact moment that Fei saw his daughter. The old man sent his eldest son to fetch his daughter the very same day and had her remarried. Fei passed the examinations the following year. He later reached the rank of Grand Master and served as the prefect of Badong [Fengjie, Sichuan]. (*YJZ, bing*:3.384.)

41 • Ma Shuyin

At age eighteen, Ma Shuyin accompanied his father, Sufu, to relocate and serve in the capital, where Shuyin died from an illness. Shuyin had an older sister who was married to the Court Gentleman of Adhering to Righteousness, Li Shu, a tax officer in Changzhou [in Jiangsu]. Shuyin's mother was staying at his sister's and did not know that her son had died. Suddenly, a maid of the Lis acted as if she had gone crazy and spoke in a man's voice, "I am Ma Shuyin. I died on a certain day in a certain month from an illness. It has been several months now. I wanted to see my mother and my older sister, so I hitchhiked on a boat to come here, hoping to beg for Buddhist offerings from you to aid in my rebirth."

When Shuyin's mother and sister first heard about what the maid had said, they were both sad and shocked. Upon questioning the maid, they were convinced that it was indeed Shuyin who had possessed the maid, and agreed to his request. The maid then stopped talking. The mother and sister subsequently called the monks at the Taiping Monastery to chant sutras, prepare a ritual banquet, and write prayers as offerings. The next day, the maid spoke again, "I am obliged to Mother and Sister for what you have done. It is a pity that one monk stopped at reading the sutra at such-and-such place and another similarly stopped at such-and-such place, so the beneficence of the service was not satisfactory." His mother did not completely believe him, so tried to confirm Shuyin's words by calling in the monks and chiding them. Both were embarrassed and apologized before they left. The mother and sister then quickly had more sutras chanted for Shuyin. (*YJZ, bing*:7.426)

42 • Xie Qi's Wife

Xie Qi lived in the village of Qilidian, south of a pond in Yushan County in Xinzhou [Shangrao, Jiangxi]. His wife was unfilial to her mother-in-law. She would often feed her mother-in-law barley, and even failed to give her enough of it, while she herself ate white rice. On the seventh day of the seventh month in the thirtieth year of the Shaoxing reign period [1161], the woman and her husband both went out, leaving the mother-in-law to watch the house. An itinerant Buddhist monk passed by the gate and begged for food from the mother-in-law. The old woman smiled and said, "I do not even have enough food to feed myself. How could I have any for you?" The monk, pointing at the rice in the pot, said, "Offer this to me." The mother-in-law shook her hand and said, "The white rice is for my daughter-in-law. I do not dare to touch it. Otherwise, I would be scolded and humiliated when she returns." The monk insisted on asking for it, but the mother-in-law did not dare to give it to him.

When the daughter-in-law came back a short while later, the monk went straight to her to ask for the rice. The woman became furious, vilifying and scolding the monk. The monk begged even more earnestly. The woman barked angrily at him and said, "Take off your robe. You can exchange it for the rice." The monk immediately took off the robe and gave it to the woman, who examined it closely and put it on herself playfully. The monk then suddenly disappeared. The robe turned into cowhide and was too tight for her to get out of. First, a patch of hair grew on the daughter-in-law's chest. It then spread to her entire body; her head and face turned into those of a cow. Her husband ran to tell the woman's parents, who rushed to their daughter's house. By that time, she had completely turned into a cow. Presently, nobody knows if she is alive or dead. *I heard this and the above three stories from Wang Riyan.* (*YJZ, bing*:8.430–31)

43 • Li Ji's Boiled Chicken

Fan Yinbin arrived in Lin'an [Hangzhou, Zhejiang] from Changsha [in Hunan] to await an official appointment. He was drinking wine with guests on the Shengyang Tower, when a boiled chicken peddler bowed to Fan twice and presented to Fan all the chicken he had. Fan looked at the person and recognized that it was his former servant, Li Ji, who had been dead for several years. Shocked, Fan asked, "Are you not Li Ji?" The peddler answered, "Yes." "You have died and become a ghost. How come you are back to life?" Ji said, "There are many like me in the world. It is only that people do not recognize us." Pointing to someone sitting on the tower and someone walking on the street, he said, "They are both my peers. We mix with humans, working as merchants, peddlers, and hired laborers, but we never do harm. Here is not the only place that has ghosts. The old woman Zhao that your family has been using for washing and cleaning is also a ghost. When you return home, ask her. She surely will deny and decline." He then reached for two small stones from his pocket, gave them to Fan, and said, "Show her these. They will cause her original form to manifest immediately." Fan asked, "The chicken you cook, is it edible?" Ji answered, "If it was not, how would I dare present it to you?" Ji left after a long while.

Fan hid the stones and went home. He told his wife, Miss Han, what he had learned. Han said, "Old Lady Zhao has been in and out of our house for twenty years. How could we treat her as a ghost? Another day, when Zhao came, Fan said jokingly, "I heard that you are a ghost. Is it true?" Upset, Zhao said, "I have associated with your family for a long time. Do not kid around." Fan said, "Li Ji told me that you are." He then showed Zhao the stones. Zhao's colors changed. Suddenly, there was a sound like that of silk being torn apart. And Zhao was nowhere to be seen. This story resembles those recorded in fiction. This is because the techniques that the ghosts use are the same. *This and the above stories were told by Tang Shaoliu.* (*YJZ, bing*:9.443)

44 • Tilers of Changshu

Grand Master of the Palace, Wu Wenyan, was a native of Dezhou [in Shandong]. He served as a prefect several times and later lived in Changshu County in Pingjiang [Suzhou, Jiangsu]. Wu had just had a residence built. Every night, he would dream of seven men, all in white clothes, coming down from the roof ridge. He told his family about the dream, but nobody knew what omen it was. Not long after, Wu fell ill and died.

His son wished to investigate the cause of the strange occurrence, so he ordered laborers to climb to the rooftop, remove the tiles, and look all over. The workers found seven paper-cut human figures in the ridge, left there by the tilers. Unhappy with their commission, the tilers must have intended to use this sorcerous technique to harm the owner of the house.

At the time, Wang Xiandao (courtesy name Huan) was the prefect. When he heard about the incident, he had all the tilers [involved in this crime] arrested and put in prison. All of them were flogged and exiled to remote prefectures.

The custom of the Suzhou region is such that, when tiles are laid, even if it is during the hottest times, young men in the family are sent to the roof to supervise the tilers. This is because families are afraid that tilers might attempt what they did to the Wus. Wu Wenyan was a northerner and did not know this custom. This was why he was fooled by the tilers' evil scheme. (*YJZ, bing*.10.452)

[handwritten note: Zhu's family wetnurse died no-one buried the bones. Appeared in dreams and then was moved locations and happier.]

45 • The Zhus' Old Wet Nurse

Zhu Hanchen from my hometown was an official in the Imperial University during the Xuanhe reign period [1119–1125]. The family's wet nurse died in the capital and was temporarily buried at a Buddhist temple.

Before he returned to his hometown, Zhu did not get to cremate her bones.[21]

The younger brother of Zhu's wife, Li Yuanchong (courtesy name Jingshan) had gone to the capital and stayed at an inn, where he dreamt about an old lady walking back and forth in his room. He had the same dream the next night. In the dream, the woman told him while sobbing, "I am the Zhus' wet nurse and unfortunately died away from home. I am now buried at such-and-such temple in such-and-such ward. It is extremely inconvenient for me to live there. I hope that you will take me home." Li asked, "There are many temporary graves there. How is yours marked?" The old lady said, "Mine is on the western side of the temple. There are two bamboos planted on my tomb. The one on the south is taller and the one on the north is shorter. The characters inscribed on the coffin are still there. If you look for them, you should be able to find them."

Li woke up and could not go back to sleep. He quickly fetched paper and brush to write down everything he had dreamt about. Later, when it was light, he went to visit the temple and found the place where the wet nurse was buried. Everything appeared as she had described.

Li informed the monk-in-residence of the matter before he had the coffin dug out and the body cremated. He then had the ashes wrapped up and handed them to a servant. The monk said, "Hundreds of people are buried here. When I first came, I would hear singing, laughing, and bantering every night. It often ended with sighing and weeping. At dawn, sacrificial utensils often changed places. It was especially rowdy on nights when the moon came out. It was almost impossible to sleep peacefully. It has been a long time since then. I am not afraid anymore."

Li later returned to Poyang [in Jiangxi]. Three days before his arrival, Zhu dreamt about the old lady visiting him. With a happy look on her face, she said, "I stayed in a strange place for a long time and was very lonely. Thanks to your brother-in-law, I am finally home. We will be arriving soon." The entire family sighed sorrowfully and sent people to welcome them on the road. They buried her with a grand Buddhist service. (*YJZ, bing*:11.456)

---

21. Cremation, a Buddhist practice, was extremely popular in the Song for a variety of reasons, among which were the widespread devotion to the Buddhist religion, the low cost of cremation, and the convenience it afforded those who moved about frequently and extensively.

46 • Jin Junqing's Wife

The daughter of a prefect in Jingnan [Jiangling, Hubei] was eighteen years old. She had been engaged and was waiting to have a date selected for the wedding ceremony when the girl dreamt about someone telling her, "The man you are engaged to is not your husband. You husband will be Jin Junqing." When she woke up, the girl did not tell her dream to anyone. She simply embroidered the three characters of Jin Junqing's name on every inch of the embroidered belt [that she was making]. Seeing what she did, her mother became suspicious and told her father. The father subsequently looked in the prefecture, all the way down to the petty officials and clerks, but found no one named Jin Junqing. The father then asked his daughter, who told him everything she had learned from the dream. Not long after that, the girl's fiancé died.

Half a year later, the new prefect of Xiazhou [Yichang, Hubei] passed by the Jingnan Prefecture and sent a calling card to the prefect's residence. The name of the new prefect was Jin Junqing. It was not until then that the girl's parents understood the earlier events. When Jin Junqing arrived, they received him generously and had him stay for days. Upon hearing that Jin had just lost his wife, the girl's parents told Jin her dream. Jin said, "I am already forty-two. Compared to your virtuous daughter, I am double her age and six years older. Besides, it has not been long since I mourned my wife. I cannot bear to do this based on the principle of righteousness." His hosts insisted on marrying their daughter to him, saying, "Marriage is determined by destiny. How could you decline it?"

Jin had no alternative but to marry the girl. He died thirty years later. His wife gave birth to several sons. Jin reached the rank of Director in the Ministry of Revenue. He was a native of Poyang [in Jiangxi]. *This and the above stories were told by Li Binwang.* (*YJZ, bing*:13.477)

47 • Jiang Ji's Horse

In the fall of the seventh year of the Qiandao reign period [1171], there was a great famine. Jiangxi and Hunan suffered especially greatly. Many people died from starvation. In the spring of the eighth year [1172], the government at Shaozhou [Shaoguan, Guangdong] sent a petty official, Jiang Ji, to go to the Yue Market at Mount Heng [in Hunan] to purchase mirabilite [Glauber's salt] and other ingredients used for making armor. Jiang Ji traveled by horse. Along the way, his horse trampled on local residents' wheat fields. Jiang also fed the horse with rice [which was inappropriate during a famine]. On the twenty-seventh day of the second month, he arrived at Yuegang within the borders of Mount Heng. Suddenly the sky turned so dark that one could see neither people nor objects. Peals of thunder rumbled loudly. Only after a long while did the sky clear. Both Jiang Ji and his horse had fallen on the ground and died. The authorities at Shaozhou reported the matter to the Fiscal Commission. The Administrative Assistant of the Commission, Chen Conggu, subsequently put up posters along the road to warn against similar violations. (*YJZ, ding*:4.566)

48 • Shi Yi Paying Back Debt in His Next Life

The monk-doctor Shi Yi in Jianyang [in Fujian] often owed people money. He once borrowed ten strings of cash coins from the county clerk Liu He. Liu asked Shi Yi to return the money many times, but Shi refused to pay back. Angered, Liu said, "I will allow you to pay back your debt in the next life." From then on, Liu never mentioned the debt again.

Five years later, Shi Yi died. Two more years had passed when Liu's mother dreamt about him visiting just like old times. Lowering his head, Shi Yi said, "I previously owed your son ten strings of cash coins. I am paying it back today with sincerity." Shi Yi left after saying these words.

The mother woke up and told Liu her dream, wondering, "What omen is this?" At dawn, a tenant came to report to them, "Last night at midnight, the white cow gave birth to a calf." (*YJZ, ding*:5.575)

49 • China Fir at the Chens' Graveyard

There was a China fir tree at the side of Chen Pu's ancestral graveyard in Jianyang [in Fujian]. The tree was huge. In the *renshen* year of the Shaoxing reign period [1152], the twelve branches of the Chen clan sold the tree to Wang Yi in the same village at a price of thirteen thousand cash coins. The two parties had agreed to cut the tree down the next day following sacrificial offerings at the burial ground.

That night, Chen Pu dreamt about several old men [i.e., earth gods] with white beards telling him, "We have been in charge of this tree for three hundred and eighty years. It is supposed to be used for the outer coffin of Mr. Huang of the Investigation Bureau. How could you cut it down as you please?" Pu asked, "Who is Huang of the Investigation Bureau?" The old men answered, "It is Prefect Huang of the Zhaoxian Ward." Pu said, "He currently lives in Xinzhou [Shangrao, Jiangxi]. Why must his family come here to look for material for his coffin?" The old men replied, "If you do not believe us, you will surely get involved in lawsuits. Besides, we have been protecting the tree for years. Even if you are determined to sell it, the deal will not work out."

Pu woke up and told his wife about the dream. The wife said, "Because of the tree, your nephews and grandsons already resent you. Do not speak carelessly about the dream." The next day, Wang Yi brought money, wine, and ducks and geese to offer sacrifices at the graveyard. When the ceremony was over, he and others gathered for a drink at Pu's house. When the party finished drinking, each of the twelve Chen branch houses received a thousand and eighty cash coins, with a surplus of forty. Pu took the leftover money and said, "This should be used to pay me for the firewood that I provided to cook the food we just consumed." One nephew was violent and malicious by nature. He snatched the money from Pu and threw it on the ground. Angered, Pu beat the nephew so badly that his foot was broken.

Wang Yi had not yet left at the time of the fight. Fearing that this would cause a lawsuit, he no longer wanted to purchase the tree and simply requested his money back from everyone. Four people refused to return the money, which led to more fighting. So all went to appeal at the county office. Originally, each of the Chen houses had twenty to thirty *mu* [about 3.5 to 5 acres] of land. All of their wealth was exhausted due to the lawsuit. Some houses even ended up moving to other counties.

Five years after the incident, Huang of the Investigation Bureau died in Xinzhou. His son Dewan was unable to find an outer coffin there, so looked for one in their hometown. Someone mentioned the Chens' China fir, saying, "The family has been wanting to sell it for a long time. But because of a dispute over forty cash coins, several of the Chen houses wasted all their assets on a lawsuit. I am afraid they may not be able to reach an agreement soon." Huang sent someone to make an inquiry anyway. It turned out, three days earlier, the Chens, who had moved away, happened to have returned. The clan had grown into sixteen branch families by now. Each was offered a thousand cash coins. All were pleased to approve the transaction. Surprisingly, the China fir did end up being used as Huang's outer coffin [as was predicted by the old men in Pu's dream].

It was not until then that Pu told everyone the dream he had years ago. Dewan counted the tree's growth rings. It was exactly over three hundred and eighty rings. Huang of the Investigation Bureau's name was Daru. (*YJZ, ding*:6.585–86)

50 • Ye Defu

Ye Defu of Jian'an [Jian'ou, Fujian] lost his parents at a young age. He only had his paternal grandmother to raise and look after him. She also did her best to make a living for her and her grandson. The grandmother once told Ye, "A fortune-teller said that you would become an official. I want to find a woman of the imperial clan to be your wife."

In the third year of the Jianyan reign period [1129], Ye and his grand-mother moved to the prefectural capital to escape bandits, who later took the city. At the time, Ye was already twenty-one and his grandmother seventy. Since she could not walk, she gave all her savings, including about seventy ounces of gold and fifty ounces of silver ingots, to Ye, asking him and two maids to get out of the city first. Before they left, the grandmother urged Ye, "You come back to take me with you. Do not desert me. Otherwise, even if I die, I will haunt you in the underworld." In the end, Ye did not come back. His grandmother subsequently died at the hands of the bandits.

When the chaos ended, it was impossible for Ye to look for and locate his grandmother's whereabouts. Ye used her funds to buy land to grow and sell tea. His wealth grew day by day. In the eighth year of the Shaoxing reign period [1138], Ye took advantage of certain situations and was selected as a tribute scholar at the prefectural-level examinations. He later married a woman from the imperial clan and received the title of the Court Gentleman for Ceremonial Service.

The next year, Ye went to participate in the Departmental Examinations at the capital. On the second day of the seventh month, he called on the Sichuanese Han Zao to inquire about his fortune [in the examinations]. Han said, "You will surely become an official, even if you do not study. If you want to ask about your future, come back twenty-two days later at the Beginning of Autumn.[22] I will tell your fortune in detail then."

Ye was extremely angry, almost to the extent of wanting to beat and humiliate Han. Huang Dewan, who accompanied Ye, persuaded him to leave. Sixteen days later, Ye fell ill. He began to genuinely worry about his health when he started to vomit blood. At the time, a monk, a fellow towns-man, came to the capital to sell tea. The monk was of the same age as Ye. Ye subsequently asked the monk to prepare both of their zodiac signs and had the monk visit Han. Upon seeing the information, Han said, "I remember telling the fortune of the first person at the beginning of the month. He would not live beyond the Beginning of Autumn. If he does not die on that day, I will never practice fortune-telling."

---

22. In traditional China, the year was divided into twenty-four solar terms (*jieqi*) of approximately fifteen days each. Each term was given a name reflecting the changes apparent in the natural world at the time of its occurrence. The year starts with the Beginning of Spring and ends with the Greater Cold. The Beginning of Autumn is the thirteenth of the twenty-four terms and usually falls on August 7 or 8.

The monk returned but did not dare to tell Ye what Han had said. While sick, Ye often whined sadly, "Tell grandmother, I will pay back her money. I would like to beg for my life to return home. Do not cut me into slices." He actually died on the day of the Beginning of Autumn [as Han had predicted].

Ye was unfilial and unrighteous. He deserved to be executed by ghosts and spirits. It was not unfortunate for him to die away from home. How miraculous are Han's fortune-telling skills! (*YJZ, ding*:6.587–88)

51 • A Questionable Lawsuit in Dayu

Li Siniang, the wife of Huang Jie, a clerk in Dayu County [in Jiangxi], had been having an illicit affair. Once, when Huang Jie left the house, she took advantage of the opportunity and went to meet her lover. The two ran away, taking with them her three-year-old son. Not long after they took off, the son started to cry and would not stop, so Li Siniang deserted him in the grass.

Li San, a runner at the county office, happened to pass by while on some official business. Seeing the boy moving about on the ground, Li could not bear to leave him there, so he carried the boy home. Li's entire family was pleased with what he did.

When Huang Jie returned home and did not see his wife and son, he looked for them thoroughly. Li San, who lived a few miles away, was holding the boy and playing with him when Huang Jie came. Huang Jie immediately told Li's neighbors [that Li had stolen his son]. Together, Huang and the neighbors seized Li and dragged him to the county office. Li was interrogated very harshly and succumbed to false charges, confessing that, "I did not have a son, so I killed Huang's wife, sank her body in the river, and stole the boy and brought him home. Now that I am caught, I am willing to be executed without any regrets."

The circumstances of the case were fully established. Li was about to be sent to the prefectural office by the county authorities. He was standing in the court in shackles when dark clouds suddenly appeared, followed by thunder and lightning. Li's shackles loosened themselves, and he stood in a trance. When everything settled slightly, the investigating clerk lay dead, with red characters on his back that appeared to mean that this was an unjust verdict. The twenty or so clerks nearby had all lost their scarves. The magistrate was similarly horrified.

A long while later, the magistrate called upon Li to state what he saw [in the chaos]. Li said, "It was pitch dark in front of my eyes; I did not know where I was. There was only one official sitting in a green gauze tent." The magistrate was terrified [of the spiritual intervention] and regretted his decision; he quickly had Li released, but Siniang and the adulterer were never caught. This happened on the twenty-ninth day of the eighth month of the nineteenth year of the Shaoxing reign period [1149]. Huang Jie, Li San, and the boy are all well now. (*YJZ, ding*:7.598–99)

52 • The Qiantang Tidal Surges

The tidal surges on the Qiantang River are the greatest on the eighteenth day of the eighth month of the lunar calendar and are extraordinary spectacles under Heaven. The custom in Lin'an [Hangzhou, Zhejiang] is that over half of the inhabitants would go to watch the tides. In the fall of the tenth year of the Shaoxing reign period [1140], two nights before the spectacle, some residents living near the river heard a voice in the air: "This year, those who are destined to die on the bridge will number in the hundreds. They are all violent, illicit, and unfilial people. We should dispatch messengers to urge those who are on the register to die but are not planning on attending to come to watch the tides and to prevent those who are not listed from coming." The residents then heard many answering the call. Feeling the incident bizarre and out of fear, they did not dare to talk about it.

The next night, someone living next to the Kuapu Bridge dreamt about someone coming to warn him, "Do not step on the bridge tomorrow. The bridge is going to break." In the morning, he told the dream to several neighbors. It turned out they all had a similar dream. Everyone sensed danger and was terrified.

By the time the tidal surges approached, spectators had already filled the bridge. Those who had the dream, [worrying about the bridge falling apart,] did not step on it but waited nearby. When they saw relatives and acquaintances standing on the bridge, they would quietly persuade them to come down. The relatives and acquaintances, however, did not take the warnings seriously. None of them would listen.

The tides arrived in short order. They sprang and gushed abnormally; terrifying waves hit the shore. The bridge was damaged from the shocks and collapsed into the water. Hundreds were overpowered by the surges and drowned.

After the incident, family members came to encoffin the bodies of the dead while wailing. Passersby pointed at the bodies and said, "These people were all wayward sorts when they were alive." It was not until then did people understand that the divinities had used the tidal surges to punish the evil and cause their deaths. The disaster was not an accident. (*YJZ, ding*:9.614)

53 • Chen Shisi and His Son

Villager Chen Shisi in Xingguo County of Ganzhou [in Jiangxi] was extremely unfilial toward his mother. He once had a dispute with his neighbor, then secretly colluded with his wife to get his mother into a fight with the neighbor. His mother had been suffering from eye problems and was old. She could not bear the jostling and grabbing and died during the altercation. Chen and his wife subsequently brought a lawsuit to the county government, falsely claiming that their mother was beaten and murdered by their neighbor. Neighbors and his sister both testified that the accusation was false. The county government subsequently took Chen to prison. He died before he was tortured. This happened in the sixth year of the Qiandao reign period [1170].

Three years later, Chen's wife was crossing a creek on her way to visit her married daughter when she was shaken by thunder and struck to death in the water by lightning. Upon hearing the news, her son ran to the stream.

Picking a long vine, he went into the stream to tie up his mother's body to pull it out. People on the bank tried to persuade the son to carry his mother's body on his back.[23] But he would not listen. There was again thunder. The son was similarly struck to death. The family line thus became extinct. *Country magistrate Mu Huai told this story.* (*YJZ, ding:*12.638)

54 • Ji Huizhi's Wife

Ji Huizhi was the county magistrate of Pingjiang in Yuezhou [Yueyang, Hunan] and a native of Huyang in Tangzhou [Tanghe, Henan]. He first married Miss Wang, the younger sister of Wang Lun of the Bureau of Military Affairs. When Miss Wang died, he remarried, to a Miss Zhang of the same prefecture. The couple lived in Changsha.

Several days after Miss Zhang gave birth to a baby girl, she became critically ill. The doctor was unable to cure her. Huizhi's mother was deeply worried and invited an old, female exorcist to examine Miss Zhang. The exorcist said, "Miss Wang, [your son's deceased wife] is standing in front of Miss Zhang, causing her great mischief." The mother ordered that a spirit tablet be set up and prayers offered to release Miss Wang's spirit. She also promised sacrificial ceremony to repent. Still Miss Wang refused to leave.

The exorcist then told Huizhi, "You must imitate what living couples do, to break off relations with Miss Wang by giving her a divorce paper. Only then will Miss Zhang be freed from her haunting." Huizhi could not bear to follow this advice. But Miss Zhang's illness became more critical by the day. Seeing that he had no alternative, Huizhi wept. Picking up the brush, he composed a divorce paper and gave it to the exorcist. The exorcist mixed the document with some paper money, then burned everything

---

23. Presumably, neighbors were trying to convince the son to show his mother the respect that she deserved from her son. Because the son refused to carry his mother's body, he was struck to death by lightning, indicating that he was partially responsible for the demise of the family line.

to have the divorce paper delivered to Miss Wang. The exorcist reported, "[When Miss Wang received the document,] she picked it up and opened it. Upon reading the divorce paper, she wailed bitterly and departed." Sure enough, Miss Zhang subsequently recovered from her illness. A living person divorcing his dead wife, this was never heard of in ancient times. Miss Zhang and my wife are cousins. She is still alive. (*YJZ*, *ding*:12.639)

55 • Mr. Hu's Wife

A Master Hu was from a rich family in Weishi County [in Henan]. He married the daughter of the Zhang family after losing his first wife. Miss Zhang was a jealous person. Hu had acquired a nun as his concubine and had her hidden away from his house for a long time. When Zhang learned about it, she called her husband home, scolding him angrily and pushing and shoving him. She even attempted to blind Hu with ashes from the stove. Hu broke free and fled, saying, "You hurt me with your beating. How outrageous this is!"

Miss Zhang became even more furious. Dashing into the yard, she roared with rage and threw herself about. At the time, Zhang was over eight months pregnant. Extremely exhausted [from fighting with her husband], she lay on the ground and fell into a lethargic sleep. In her sleep, Zhang dreamt about Hu's first wife coming to her and saying, "He is my husband. How could you dare to possess him? I am going to kill your child now." The first wife then raised her fist to hit Zhang's belly.

Miss Zhang woke up from her dream, trembling with fear. She told people what she had seen in the dream. By the time she went back to the bedroom, the pain in her belly had become unbearable. The family lived forty *li* [about twenty kilometers or thirteen miles] away from the county seat. They rushed to send for an obstetrician. Before the doctor arrived, however, the fetus fell to the ground and died. (*YJZ*, *ding*:12.640)

56 • The Pomegranate Tree at Hanyang

In the early years of the Shaoxing reign period [1131–1162], there was a widow in Hanyang Commandery [in Hubei] who was very devoted to her mother-in-law. The mother-in-law died without having fallen ill. Neighbors subsequently falsely incriminated the daughter-in-law for poisoning the mother-in-law and brought a lawsuit against her at the government office. The daughter-in-law could not stand the interrogation and torture and confessed to the crime. When she was about to leave the prison to be executed, the prison guard put a pomegranate flower on her hair bun. By the time they reached the market, [which also served as the execution ground,] the daughter-in-law said to the executioner, "Take this flower and insert it into the stone cracks on the slope for me." She then prayed, "I did not actually murder my mother-in-law. If Heaven is watching, let this flower grow into a tree. If I am guilty, this flower will wither in a day." Those who had heard the prayers all pitied her. The woman then was executed. The next day, the flower had already grown new leaves. It eventually became a tree and grew to over three feet tall. To this day, it has borne fruit every year. (*YJZ*, *ding*:13.647)

57 • Dongpo's Snow Hall[24]

He Hu of Huangzhou [in Hubei] was the son of He Jie (courtesy name Siju), a disciple of Dongpo [i.e., Su Shi, 1037–1101]. After the war [between the Song and the Jin in the late 1020s] ended, He lived temporarily on an island in Ezhou [in Hubei] and would return to visit Huangzhou around

---

24. Dongpo was the courtesy name of Su Shi (1037–1101), a major literary, political, and intellectual figure of the Northern Song. Su Shi acquired the name Dongpo, East Slope, while living in exile in Huangzhou (in Hubei) in the 1080s. In addition to building the Snow Hall, Su Shi had a small bridge built and personally planted a willow tree while in Huangzhou. All of these physical traces remained celebrated sites in Huangzhou after Su's departure.

the Cold Food Festival every spring. In the year *wuwu* of the Shaoxing reign period [1138], the prefect of Huangzhou, Han Zhimei, rebuilt [Dongpo's] Snow Hall as a way to preserve the physical traces that Su had left behind. It was mid-spring at the time. He Hu happened to be visiting. In a dream, Dongpo told him, "The foundation of Snow Hall is 120 *bu* [720 feet] away] from my original site. The Small Bridge and Slim Willow Tree are not in their original locations either. You should correct these." He Hu tried to remember each detail of what Dongpo had said in the dream. The next day he went to tell [Prefect] Han. Han changed everything per He's instructions. Another day, an eighty-seven-year-old man named Tang Deming came to visit from Huangbo. On seeing the Snow Hall, Tang sighed, "This is exactly where Academician Su laid the foundation of the Snow Hall." *Prefect Han told this story and the previous one.* (*YJZ, ding*:18.690)

58 • Monk Ding in Xujiang

In the early years of the Shaoxing reign period [1131–1162], a monk passed by the Huangs' inn, fifteen *li* [about 12.5 kilometers or 5 miles] north of Xujiang [Guangchang, Jiangxi]. Imposing both in figure and appearance, the monk introduced himself to Huang, "My secular family name is Ding." Several days later, the monk told Huang, "I will go into town to beg, but will return in the evening." For several months, the monk would give a portion to Huang of whatever money and things that he received from begging. Huang subsequently treated the monk as a special guest. For a long time, the monk continued to stay at the inn. Huang was no longer suspicious whenever the monk came and went.

Occasionally, the monk would hit on Huang's wife, who was young and good looking; the woman already liked the monk's appearance. Besides, because she had received money from the monk several times, in her heart, she had already tacitly consented to his advances, yet still pretended to reject him. One day when it was dark, the wife came into the monk's room. There was no lamp in there, but it was naturally light. The monk had on him a gold-laced robe and sat on a green lotus flower on the wall. He looked exactly like the Buddha or Bodhisattva portrayed in Buddhist paintings. Stunned and in admiration, Huang's wife bowed to him. The monk quickly jumped off his lotus pedestal and told her, "I am not human. I will redeem you. You shall not let the secret out." He then kept her in the room and had illicit sexual relations with her.

From then on, whenever her husband went out, the woman would go to see the monk. This went on for a long time. Eventually Huang learned about the affair and confronted his wife. She did not dare to hide the truth, so she told him everything. Huang was furious and planned to have the monk arrested and punished. He pretended to go out of town and would stay overnight but came back secretly. After people had settled in for the night, his wife went to inform the monk, "My husband wishes to capture you. What are you to do?" The monk said, "Do not worry about it." He then closed the door and went to bed.

Huang was hiding outside the door, eavesdropping. Upon hearing the monk and his wife talking, Huang became even more infuriated. He wanted to break into the room but was not able to. The only thing he could do was to yell and curse at the monk. At first, the monk would respond, but soon his voice sounded more and more distant. A short while later, it became completely silent inside. Huang destroyed a wall to enter and lit a torch to light up the room; it was already empty. The four walls were all bare. The monk, Huang's wife, and all the things in the room were nowhere to be seen. But the windows, walls, doors, and locks were all intact. Huang gathered his neighbors, looking for the monk and his wife until it was light, but to no avail. In the end, no one knew where they went. *Huang Yanzhong, a recluse at the Chongzhen Shrine in Jianchang [Nancheng, Jiangxi], told this story.* (*YJZ, ding*:19.694–95)

59 • Xie's Efficacious Mandarin Oranges

The mother of Xie of Wenzhou [in Zhejiang] was old and ill but refused to take medicine. In the summer, she craved mandarin oranges as much as she did water and food when she was thirsty and hungry. Xie was at his wit's end about his mother's request. The family had a small garden, in which there was a mandarin orange tree. Xie therefore prayed under the tree at night. He knelt there for so long that his knees cracked. By the morning, the tree had already grown several pieces of the orange fruit. Xie picked the fruit, presenting them to his mother while kneeling on the ground. As soon as his mother ate the fruit, her old illness was cured.

Those who heard about Xie's deeds proclaimed them as the manifestation of his filial devotion to his mother. Scholar-officials from far and near contended to write poems, lyrics, and songs to praise Xie's virtue. Their compositions were collected and entitled "Scroll of Poems on the Efficacious Mandarin Oranges." The prefect Wang Gai (courtesy name Xunze) circulated the collection in other places, further praising and promoting Xie's behavior. It is a pity that the compositions were not presented to the court and recorded in official historical documents. That way, Xie would follow the path of Jiang Shi and Meng Zong to reach immortality.[25] The miracle happened in the fourteenth year of the Chunxi reign period [1186]. (*YJZ, ding:*19.700)

---

25. Both Jiang Shi and Meng Zong were filial exemplars in history. Jiang Shi of the Han (202 BCE–220 CE) was known to walk a great distance every day to fetch water from a river because the water had a sweet taste. His mother liked a particular fish dish; both he and his wife made sure to get the fish for the mother. Their filial behavior eventually moved Heaven and a spring appeared next to their house. Its water tasted just like that from the river, sparing them the task of fetching it from a long distance. The spring also produced two carp every day for the mother's consumption. Meng Zong lived in the Jin (266–420). Having lost his father when he was a boy, Meng Zong did not know what to do when his mother was sick and craved bamboo shoots in the winter. So he went off to wail in the bamboo woods. His filial sentiments moved Heaven and Earth and new bamboo shoots grew. Meng used them to cook a soup, which cured his mother.

60 • The Old Lady of Wushan

In the *xinmao* year of the Qiandao reign period [1171], Wushan Village in Xinjian [Nanchang, Jiangxi] suffered from a famine and an epidemic. One farmer's family had more than ten people; all perished except for an old lady and her grandson. The old lady also died soon. Upon her passing, the grandson overcame his own illness to get out of the house. Despondently, he implored neighbors to help him bury his grandmother. Fearing that they might contract the disease, nobody was willing to assist the grandson.

Five days later, the old lady's hands and feet moved slightly. Her body soon became warm and her eyes opened. She came back to life. The grandson helped the grandmother sit up and asked, "Where were you the last several days? If neighbors had been willing to help, you would have been buried. Fortunately, they did not come to assist me. Was this not Heaven's will?" The old lady said, "I did not know any of this. The only thing I saw was that someone called me to go with him. I followed him, carrying my old traveling basket. When we reached a bridge, someone came down from it, ordering me to leave my luggage there. He then told me to walk on the bridge. Looking around, I saw many people treading in water and mud. When they lifted their feet, it was as if their feet were stuck. I did not have the time to ask why before we arrived at a government office. The office's red doors were wide open. Inside the doors, people wore red and purple caps and robes. Many men and women in black and yellow were being chased around. I ran into a county clerk that I used to know and asked him where we were. The clerk said, 'This is not what you should know, nor are you supposed to be here; these are all people who are destined to suffer this catastrophe. There is a minor catastrophe every five hundred years [during which many die]. I oversee the registers that are made of *ling* silk, *juan* silk, and paper. The paper register has all been marked. So is half of the *juan* register. You are on the *juan* register, but it is not your time to die yet; you should go back immediately.' The clerk had someone lead me out. I again crossed the bridge, where the guard greeted and said to me, 'Here is your traveling basket. Since you have a merciful heart, you have been spared this calamity. I am happy for you. Go home now to save your family.' I then slipped, fell under the bridge, and came back to life." *Qi Che told this story.* (*YJZ, ding*:20.707–8)

61 • The Wife of Master Zhang

Qian Lüdao (courtesy name Jiazhen) was a native of Xianyang in Jingzhao [Xi'an, Shaanxi]. In the Huangtong reign period [1141–1148] during the Jurchen's rule, he studied away from his hometown in Shang [in Shaanxi] and Guo [Lushi, Henan]. Once, while passing through Hu County [in Shaanxi], attempting to cover more distance, he did not stop in time to find lodging. At the time, he only had one servant accompanying him. It had become pitch dark and impossible to see the road, so he let the horse roam freely.

When Qian and the servant reached a large residence, he knocked on the door, intending to ask to be put up for the night. A young maid came out. Shocked to see Qian, she said, "This place is close to the mountain, which has many wolves and tigers. How is it suitable for night travel?" Qian said, "We accidentally got lost just now and would be grateful if we could stay at your place for one night. However, I do not know which high-ranking official's residence this is." The maid said, "This is the residence of the prefect of Hezhong, Master Zhang. After the master's death, only *furen* lives here.[26] I must inform her of your arrival before I give you permission to stay." Having said this, the maid went back in to report to the mistress.

A short while later, Qian was invited into the house. In giant halls and lofty rooms, bright candles were lit in front of him. Wine glasses and dishes were already laid out. *Furen* looked dignified and gorgeous and her hairpiece and clothes were splendid. She and Qian then enjoyed a banquet together. The fine quality of the maids' dancing was something that Qian had never witnessed. He considered this a wonderful encounter and felt as if he were touring a fairyland. His state of mind swayed so much that he had forgotten where he was. Bowing to each other, then sitting down courteously, he and *furen* chose their words carefully when speaking to each other. Those present all thought that they were behaving in a silly manner. They turned to look at each other, then laughed at Qian and *furen*.

When the banquet was over, Qian went to bed. In a short while, candlelight approached and *furen* entered his room. The maids stood around her

---

26. *Furen* was a term of address for married women of elevated social and political status in ancient China.

- romantic- relationship - zhang married

and helped her get into bed with Qian. Qian quickly got out of the bed to excuse himself. But the maids insisted on his staying, so Qian and *furen* slept on the same bed.

The next day, *furen* kept Qian and his servant for meals. Qian was originally a wanderer. Pleased with the physical relationship with the woman, he did not bring up leaving for days.

One night, while they were drinking happily, Qian heard from outside the window the sound of people calling, scolding, and giving directions. Someone announced, "Master is coming." *Furen* suddenly got up. The maids all rushed about and dispersed. Qian laid low in a dark room and did not even dare to gasp for air for fear of being discovered. He pretended to sleep for a long time without moving. Outside, foxes howled and crows cawed.

When there was light in the east, both the house and people were gone. Qian was alone, lying amid thistles and thorns in an ancient grave. Getting out of the grave, he felt lost and embarrassed. It was not until he ran into a farmer that he found his way back to the official road. The lingering fragrance from the woman's clothes did not disappear for a month. (*YJZ, zhijia*:1.712)

— covered in thorns with her smell still on him.

62 • General Liu

After the despised Jurchens occupied the land of Qi and Lu [in Shandong in the late 1120s], they changed the name of Fengfu County to that of Tai'an Commandery. In the second year of the Huangtong reign period [1142], it did not rain for an entire month. General Liu, a man of Han descent, was serving as the administrator at the time and went to pray for rain at the Daiyue.[27] There was no rainfall following the ceremony. Liu then sacrificed at the Dragon Pool, but the illustrious sun blazed even brighter.

---

27. Daiyue is an alternative name for Mount Tai, one of the famous Five Peaks, located in modern Shandong Province. The other four peaks are Mount Heng in Shanxi, Mount Hua in Shaanxi, Mount Song in Henan, and Mount Heng in Hunan.

Enraged [by the unresponsive deities], Liu ordered laborers to carry dirt and rocks to fill up the pool.

That night, Liu dreamt about a divinity telling him, "It is not my fault that it has not rained for a long time. At present, in all the four seas, even a single ladle of water is controlled by a deity; I do not get to intervene. How dare I violate heavenly laws to send down rain at my will? I hope you understand this!"

Liu woke up even angrier. At dawn, he led over a thousand soldiers to transport even more dirt and rocks to throw into the pool. By dusk the pool was filled. But the next morning, the pool returned to its previous state. Liu did not take this as a warning, but continued to exhaust human resources to realize his goal.

One day, it was tremendously hot; cold winds suddenly arose. Thunder and lightning came out of the pool. Mountains and hills alike all shook. Both officials and ordinary people were terrified. Still, Liu did not stop urging the laborers to continue to fill the pool. Several days later, Liu died suddenly. Rain then fell abundantly. (*YJZ, zhijia*:1.714)

63 • Qi Niangzi[28]

The currents of the Yellow River cut through the Taihang Mountains and headed east.[29] The river had dozens of steep cataracts, where the water's flow was so torrential that fish and turtles could not stay still underwater. One of these cascades was named Qi Niangzi Cataract.

At the top of the mountain [where the Qi Niangzi Cataract was], there was a shrine for the daughter of the dragon king. Thousands of families lived at the bottom of the mountain. Every year in the summer when the

---

28. Niangzi was a term of address for married women.
29. The Taihang Mountain is a large mountain range in the north central China plain, stretching across the city of Beijing and Shanxi, Hebei, and Henan Provinces.

billowing waters surged to the sky, the residents would have to build dykes and worry about their villages being submerged in water. Finally, the elders discussed the matter together and decided to move their village to some other location.

There was a scholar, Han Yuanweng, who was experienced and knowledgeable and trusted by the villagers. [Before the move,] the elders went to consult him. Yuanweng said, "We have lived here for generations. Our family graveyards and residences have been handed down for generations. If we discard these suddenly, it will be hard for us to have peace of mind. Let us first offer our sincere prayers at the dragon shrine. It would not be too late if we planned accordingly based on the outcome of the sacrifice." The villagers then collected money, prepared ceremonial animals and wine, and selected a date to visit the shrine. There they asked to move the goddess's shrine to the river bank so that it would protect the village from flooding. [This way, the residents would not have to move to another location.] The villagers divined and received an auspicious result. Everyone kowtowed and went home.

While they were worrying about the expenses of moving the shrine, thunder and winds arose that night. The sound of the thunder resembled that of falling mountains, and torrential rains poured into the river. Foxes howled and ghosts cried. People living at the bottom of the mountain all got up, thinking they must have angered the deity.

When it was dawn, the storm had cleared and everything appeared to be harmonious. The shrine for the daughter of the dragon king [had been moved from the top of the mountain] and stood on flat ground in its original form. [From the statue of the goddess] down to its foot-long rafters and numerous pieces of tiles, nothing was missing or damaged. Even the plaster on the walls and statues were in order. The shrine appeared level and straight and its foundation solid. It actually looked better than the old one. From that time on, excessive torrents would stop at the shrine. The villagers no longer had anything to worry about. (*YJZ, zhijia*:1.718–19)

64 • Old Woman Li's Grave

There was an ancient tomb within the borders of Xiapei [Xiayi, Henan]. Legend has it that it was the grave of a woman named Li. Nobody knew when she lived. It was also said that great amounts of treasures were interred in her grave. Over time, rascals and villains cast greedy eyes upon it. In the *dingsi* year of the Shaoxing reign period [1137], during the last year of the rule of the puppet state Qi in north China, banditry was rife in the region.[30] Not a single day would pass without the bandits burning down houses and looting graves. They finally turned to Old Woman Li's tomb.

The bandits gathered three hundred people and prepared scoops and shovels as tools. From morning until midday, they broke the ground and continued to dig, eventually reaching the grave's passage. Both the inner and outer coffins were subsequently exposed.

Feeling tired and sleepy, some bandits lay down to rest. Others stopped to have something to eat. Just then, a tall old lady appeared. She had white hair and a dark complexion and was extremely ugly. Wearing a loose, white silk robe, she sat upright on the outer coffin. She then snapped her finger and let out a long whistling sound, which echoed through the forests and valleys. Streams and rivers all boiled over and gushed forth. The bandits were horrified and quickly dispersed.

Instantly, mists and clouds closed in from all directions. Spirits and ghosts came and went. Some people heard carriages and horses, others the clapping of thunder. A few hours later, all cleared up. One bold robber went back to find out what had happened and saw that both the inner and outer coffins were nowhere to be seen; there was only an empty pit. The bandit came back sighing and regretting what he had done.

In the next fifty days or so, many who had participated in the tomb robbing either died abruptly or went insane for no reason. Villagers did their best to have the deceased buried and offered religious services. (*YJZ, zhijia*:2.722)

---

30. The Qi state referred to the short-lived regime that the Jin (1115–1234) established after it defeated the Northern Song and occupied the entire north of China in the 1120s. Headed by Liu Yu (1073–1140s), the Qi lasted from 1130 to 1137.

65 • The Shrine of Nine Dragons

The Liangs of White Dragon Valley in Tongzhou [Lingbi, Anhui] were in the trade of pottery making and metal casting for many generations. The family was extremely wealthy and over time built ten kilns, all of which produced ceramics. One kiln's products were the best. In the remaining nine kilns, however, when the fire was extinguished and the wares were taken out, they would all deflate or look irregular. When the containers were sold at the market, people nonetheless contended to buy them. It was like this every time. Liang did not understand why.

In the area, there used to be a White Dragon Shrine, which took its name from the valley. Since it did not have a reputation for being powerful, the shrine was not worshipped by many in the villages. One day, Liang dreamt about an old dragon turning into a man and visiting him. The dragon said, "I have nine sons. They are all grown up now but do not have a place to reside. They are temporarily living under your kilns. When you make pottery, they have always done their best to secretly help you." Liang said, "Ever since the nine kilns were built, they have never produced a good ware. I have always wondered why. What help from your sons are you talking about?" The dragon said, "How could you not understand? Your wares are of low quality, yet you always make a large profit. Is this not my sons' contribution?" Liang suddenly understood. He got up, bowing and expressing his gratitude to the old dragon. The dragon said, "If you could build a shrine for them, you will receive greater fortunes in the future."

Liang agreed to the dragon's request before waking up from the dream. He called for craftsmen and prepared materials for the shrine that very day. The new shrine was erected on the old site, where the statue of the old dragon was placed in its center. To the east and west, nine plaques were set up to worship his nine sons. When the shrine was completed, residents from near and far gathered to admire it, pay their respects to the dragon kings, and enjoy themselves. Another day, when they prayed there for rain due to excessive sunny days, it rained within a day. The Liangs became even richer than before. (*YJZ, zhijia*:2.725–26)

66 • Liu Chengjie's Horse

Liu Chengjie of Western Zhejiang left his position as the tax officer of Ganzhou [in Jiangxi] and was on his way to the capital for reappointment. He temporarily left his family in Ganzhou, bringing with him only a son and a servant. Riding on horseback, the three men headed east. When they reached Guixi in Xinzhou [in Jiangxi], they stopped at noon at an inn, where they ran into several merchants carrying costus roots [a medicinal herb] with them. Sitting at the same table, Liu and the merchants inquired where the other party had come from. Liu wished to purchase costus roots from the merchants, so picked up some to examine, but found the merchandise to be of low quality. He then added, "What I have in my possession is not much, but it is much better than yours." Liu then fetched his traveling trunk, taking out what he had to show the merchants. In his trunk was over a hundred ounces of silver, at which the merchants snuck a peek. It happened that dusk had fallen, so both parties stayed for the night.

The merchants were in fact bandits. Late at night, with sticks in hand, they entered Liu's room to rob Liu. Liu had previously served in the military and was strong. Wielding a knife, he cut off one of the robber's arms. Terrified by Liu, the robbers scattered and fled.

The inn owner was an accomplice of the bandits. [After the dispersal of the robbers,] he fooled Liu by saying, "Since the thieves failed to gain anything, they will surely gather others and come back. You should not relax and go back to bed. It would be better if you headed to the road to avoid the robbers before it is light." Liu did not suspect that the owner was deceiving him. He urged the servant to get up and they left without having a meal.

When Liu and his company arrived at the bottom of a deep ridge, they ran into the robbers again. Although they fought hard and tried to ward the robbers off, the three of them were fighting against hopeless odds. Liu and his son and the servant all died. A postal courier happened to pass by at the time; the robbers killed him as well. They threw the bodies in a pit, divided up what they had seized, and ran off.

Liu's horse loitered on the road. It just so happened that the assistant magistrate was on an inspection tour for land registration. [When the horse saw him,] it greeted the assistant magistrate in front of his carriage, raising its feet as if it was bowing to the official. The horse then retreated and stepped forward several times. The assistant magistrate found what the horse did strange and said, "The horse must have some injustice to recount." He subsequently sent several government office runners to follow the animal. When they arrived at the bottom of the ridge, the horse dug at the dirt and then stood still. There were blood stains everywhere and the stench was repellant. There in the pit were four corpses, still warm.

The assistant magistrate immediately urged the village head to investigate and capture the criminals. Before the end of the day, all were caught and executed. (*YJZ, zhijia*:3.730–31)

67 • Assistant Magistrate Yü

Assistant Magistrate Yü was a native of Jian'an [Jian'ou, Fujian] and a man of outstanding learning. After receiving the examination degree, he was appointed to a position in Yixing [in Jiangsu], but died just before he took office. One day later, he came back to life and said, "At first, when I was sick and at a loss, I saw a runner bowing to me in the hall, saying, 'My master desires your presence.' I then followed him. After walking for almost a hundred *li* [fifty kilometers or thirty-five miles], I could go no farther, so implored him to take a short rest. In the end, we entered a place that resembled a temple in the living world. The runner led me through the entrance, where I saw the master. He wore a crown with jade pendants and sat upright. I kowtowed and asked, 'I do not mean to refuse to die. But given that my father is old and there is no one else to care for him, I beg that you grant me time to live to the end of his allotted life span. I would then have no regrets.' The master said, 'Do you recall anything from your previous life?' I said, 'I do not.' The king said, 'Your previous name was Chen Zhaolao. In this life, you have relied on Chen's old learning, so are intelligent and enlightened without peer. But throughout your entire life, you have not done the slightest good deed. Therefore, your fortune is minimal. Sympathizing that you studied hard, the god above granted you an examination degree. The reason you did not get to earn an official salary and died young was precisely because you never did anything virtuous to accumulate good fortune. I feel sorry that you aspire to support your father, so have informed the heavenly court, which has allowed me to postpone your death for seven days. You can go home to bid your father farewell.' This was why I have been allowed to return to life." Knowing that he would not live long, Yü held his father and wept. Sure enough, he died seven days later. (*YJZ, zhijia*:3.731–32)

68 • Xiong Er Was Unfilial

Xiong Er, a resident of the Xingguo Commandary [Yangxin, Hubei], was rebellious and unreasonable by nature. His father, Ming, had been a soldier. When Ming was old, he was removed from the military registry and could not make a living to support himself. Ming's wife had died young, so Ming only had his son to rely on. However, his son, Xiong Er, treated him like a stranger, to the extent that Ming had to beg for food. Ming wept and implored sincerely that his son support him, but Xiong Er unleashed a torrent of verbal abuse on Ming and refused to listen to his father. Ming had planned to sue Xiong Er, but could not bear to go through with it in the end. Instead, he burned incense every night, praying to the gods and to Heaven that his son would come around and be filial to him. This lasted for two years.

One day, the evil son was drinking excessively and gambling with friends when the vast sky, initially cloudless, suddenly became overcast and gloomy. Rain fell violently. There came thunder and lightning. It was so dark that people standing face to face could not see each other. But they heard someone calling the name of Xiong Er.

When it cleared up a while later, Xiong Er was nowhere to be seen. Together, people looked for him and found his body outside of the city gate. His eyes were gouged out and his tongue cut. There were red characters on his back that clearly marked, "Unfilial Son." This occurred on the seventh day of the ninth month of the third year of the Chunxi reign period [1176]. (*YJZ, zhijia*:3.732–33)

69 • Li Rou

The courtesan Li Rou of Qüzhou [in Zhejiang] was highly regarded by scholar-officials who associated with her because she was clever, cunning, and excelled at singing and dancing. When she was just over twenty, she fell ill and died. Wang Xian, a runner in the prefectural government, was from the same village as Li. At the time of Li's death, Wang was on an official mission to Qiantang [in Zhejiang]. When he reached Shouchang County [Jiande, Zhejiang] on his return trip, he ran into Li on the road. Wang was surprised that Li was walking alone, so asked her, "Where are you going?" Li replied, "I am going to Lin'an [Hangzhou, Zhejiang] to watch the suburban sacrifice ceremonies." The runner asked, "Why have you not brought any maids or servants with you? Nor are you taking a sedan chair. A woman traveling a long distance alone, how could this be convenient?" Li Rou smiled but did not answer Wang's questions. When they parted, she said, "Please go to my house and tell my parents that I am having a smooth journey." Wang agreed to pass on Li's message.

When Wang returned home, he went to the Lis first. It was not until then did he realize that what he had seen on the road was Li Rou's ghost. (*YJZ, zhijia*:4.741)

70 • Defense Commissioner Xu

Luo Qinruo of Jishui in Jizhou [Jishui, Jiangxi], assistant magistrate Yang, and eye doctor Xu Yuan were sightseeing together in the wilds of the county when they ran into a traveler, who looked at them with great concentration for a long time. The three friends asked the traveler, "[Did you study our faces] because you can read physiognomy?" The person said, "Yes." They then asked him to tell their fortune. The person said to Luo, "You can reach the rank of Grand Master in the future." He then told Yang, "Your allotted official rank is mediocre, but you will gain power from your son. If you retire from officialdom early, you will be given the title of Vice Director while alive." Last he told Xu, "You are truly a highly ranked person."

The three men looked at each other and were stunned. Even the servants ridiculed the absurdity of what the fortune-teller had just said. Some made fun of the traveler, saying, "Luo and Yang are both ranked officials with examination degrees. Xu is only an eye doctor. He carried a case of books and traded his skills. Every day, his income amounts to a hundred cash coins. He has no other means to support himself. How could he become a highly ranked person?" The traveler said, "This is not something that you are capable of understanding. Only those who are close to the emperor daily can be called high officials. Mr. Xu is about to experience that." Everyone laughed and went on their way.

Later, Luo's and Yang's rankings were exactly as foretold. Xu resided in Lin'an [Hangzhou, Zhejiang] and was unhappy that he did not realize his aspirations. It so happened that the Empress Dowager Xianren suffered from an eye problem and the court intended to look for a cure from commoner doctors. As a result, Xu got to demonstrate his skills. He was subsequently granted official ranks and a residence. These were followed by countless gifts and other bestowals. He became known as the Defense Commissioner Xu. A son of his passed the examinations. (*YJZ, zhijia*:7.766–67)

71 • The Howler Zhang Er[31]

When the senior clerk Ding at Ezhou [Wuchang, Hubei Province] died, his wife was only thirty. She became sexually involved with a butcher named Zhu Si. Her son, Ding Erlang, was young and could not stop the affair. By the time Erlang was grown, Zhu showed no sign of self-restraint in front of Erlang. He and the widow would act licentiously even during the day. Zhu even resented that Erlang did not bow to him, accusing Erlang of being

---

31. The meaning of the title of this story, "Xiao Zhang Er," is not entirely clear. *Xiao* literally means "to howl" or "to breathe heavily." Here I take it to mean that Zhang Er had a bad temper. It might also be possible that he had asthma and always breathed quite heavily.

disrespectful. This was because he had begun to treat himself as Erlang's stepfather. Although angry, Ding Erlang refrained from saying anything for the sake of his mother, lest her scandalous reputation become widely known.

There was a howler named Zhang Er, who was a native of Zhucheng in Mizhou [in Shandong] and had migrated to the south in the wake of the turmoil [caused by the Jin conquest of the Northern Song]. Zhang was also a butcher by profession and was strong and brave, with a temper that was easily roused. Ding thought that he could entrust Zhang with the matter of his mother and Zhu Si. Whenever Ding was at the market drinking with his buddies, if he saw Zhang passing while carrying meat for sale, he would call Zhang over, buy from him, and pay generously. Over time, he had begun to pay Zhang as much as several times the meat's worth.

Another day, Ding invited Zhang to drink and asked why Zhang peddled wearily instead of setting up a stall in the market. Zhang said, "I peddle not because I am incapable of managing a stall. It is because I am empty handed and do not have any capital." Ding gave Zhang several hundred strings of cash coins, secretly expecting that Zhang would be grateful for his kindness and be willing to help him.

Another day, Ding asked Zhang slowly and calmly, "Did you know that I have grievances in my heart?" Zhang answered, "No. I did not." Ding then [told Zhang about the affair between his mother and Butcher Zhu] and asked Zhang to beat Zhu. Zhang responded irritably, "I was surprised when you loaned me money. Now I understand—it was because you wanted to involve me in a fight." [After finishing his words,] Zhang got up abruptly and left. After the incident, whenever they ran into each other, Zhang would act as if he did not know Ding and the two practically broke off relations. People made fun of Ding for not knowing how to judge character and for associating with someone inferior and not of his own type. Ding was also resentful of Zhang.

Not long after the confrontation [between Ding and Zhang], Zhang asked Zhu to cross the [Yangzi] River and buy hogs in Hanyang [in Hubei]. When competing for a boat, the two ended up fighting, hitting and beating each other. One night after they returned from Hanyang, Zhang entered Zhu's house, killing three people, including Zhu and his son and daughter. Zhang then tied himself up and turned himself in at the government office. Throughout the entire incident, Zhang did not mention Ding's name at all.

At the time, Junior Guardian Yue was commanding a large army in Ezhou. Considering what Zhang did to be righteous, Yue sent in an official order for

Zhang to be enlisted without punishing Zhang for the crime he had committed. Zhang was later promoted to the rank of officer due to his meritorious service. (*YJZ, zhijia*:8.772–73)

72 • Kui Liu's Mother

Kui Liu, a lowly person, lived five *li* [about 2.5 kilometers or 1.7 miles] north of town in Poyang [in Jiangxi]. His family was extremely poor, so he worked for others as a tenant laborer. In the summer of the tenth year of the Chunxi reign period [1183], Kui Liu conspired with Shi Wu of the same village to steal an ox from the Chai family during the night. Kui happened to arrive early and killed the ox with a short knife. Hearing noise outside, Chai came to the cattle pen with a stick in hand, but Kui was able to flee the scene.

Shi Wu came soon after and was beaten heavily by Chai. He returned home and died several days later. Because Shi died from stealing, his wife did not dare to inform the authorities. Thus, no one else knew about Kui's wrongdoing. He thought he had succeeded in escaping justice.

A year later, Kui's mother died from an illness but came back to life one night later. She told her son, "Previously, you and Shi Wu conspired to steal the Chais' ox. Shi was killed by Chai, but you were spared. Although your crime was not exposed in the living world, the underworld needs you to answer for this charge. You will not be spared this time." After saying this, the mother died. Three days later, Kui also died. (*YJZ, zhijia*:8.776)

73 • The Righteous Servant of Zhang Xie

Zhang Xie, a resident of Dongjian in Chuzhou [Huaiyin, Jiangsu], was extremely rich. Zhang liked to grant favors on others and was devoted to aiding the poor without expecting anything in return. In his prime, however, he suffered from the turmoil [caused by the Jin conquest of the Northern Song in the mid-1120s] and ended up wandering from place to place. Separated from his family, he temporarily settled in the Sheyang Lake area with only one servant accompanying him; the master and servant supported themselves by begging.

One day, Zhang was captured by bandits. Unable to extract any money from him, the bandits tied Zhang under a large tree and were about to eat him alive. They had already sliced some flesh off his body. Zhang's servant had fled the bandits and was free. When seeing that [his master was about to be slain], the servant came out [from his hiding place], wailing. Using his body to protect Zhang, the servant bowed to the bandits and said, "This is my master. He was originally rich and powerful, but is now fleeing from a calamity empty handed. He does not even have food to feed himself. How could he possibly have money or possessions? If you want to feed with his flesh, [he does not taste good because] he is thin and weak. Please slice me instead."

Although the bandits enjoyed killing, they were moved by the righteousness of the servant. Hearing the servant's words, they sighed in admiration of his outstanding conduct. They immediately untied Zhang and released him and the servant, even sending them off with some money and silk.

By the middle of the Shaoxing reign period [1131–1162], the Huai region stabilized. Zhang Xie returned home. His businesses and properties were still worth over a million cash coins. The servant was also alive. Zhang treated him like a brother, and Zhang's sons treated the servant like an uncle. (*YJZ, zhijia*:9.784)

74 • Chen Tiqian

The Chens of Nancheng [Mengjin, Henan] had a son, Tiqian (courtesy name Deguang). Deguang was originally a scholar, but later left home and became a Buddhist monk. Tianqian was his religious name. Tiqian was usually reckless in his behavior and loved drinking and beautiful women. After he became a monk, he did not change his old ways. Although he resided in the Bao'en Guangxiao Monastery, he would often stay at home. In addition, he would secretly rape women in the neighborhood. People all around knew of his conduct, yet Tiqian acted calm and relaxed about it. In fact, being drunk and eating meat were the least of his violations.

In the last years of the Qiandao reign period [1165–1173], Tiqian fell sick, but it had not yet become very serious. He had a dream in which he was chased to the government office. The person in charge, donning an official robe, was enraged and chided him, "Your mouth chants Buddhist sutras, but your body violates Buddhist discipline. Even death would not expiate all your crimes." The official then ordered the prison guards to put shackles on Tiqian. Tiqian repented while kowtowing with his forehead touching the ground, but the official would not hear it. Completely stunned, Tiqian woke up shaking and palpitating. He then told people what he had seen and said, "It is too late to regret what I have done." He died ten days later. (*YJZ, zhijia*:10.792)

75 • Zhai Bajie[32]

Merchants in Jiang, Huai, Min, and Chu who traveled to remote places over long periods of time often brought with them a woman to perform such tasks as cooking, preparing firewood, and fetching water.[33] At night, they would share a bed with the woman. The woman was like a concubine and was called *shenzi*. Most of them were no different from lowly prostitutes.

Throughout his life, Wang Sanke of Shangrao [in Jiangxi] traded in the Luzhou [Hefei, Anhui] and Shouzhou [Shouxian, Anhui] regions and would sometimes make two trips a year. On these trips, he had a woman,

---

32. Zhai's name literally means "Eighth older sister." *Jie*, older sister, was also used as a term of address for women from an ordinary family background.
33. Jiang, Huai, Min, and Chu referred to large areas in the middle and lower reaches of the Yangzi River in southeast China.

Zhai Bajie, living with him. Although Zhai was a woman, she was unusually strong, with her strength surpassing that of ordinary people. When traveling on the road, she would carry loads of merchandise or push the cart, making her shoulders red and her feet calloused, but she did not consider this hard work. Even strong men were no match for her.

By nature, Zhai was cunning and loved seeking profit. She was good at making money, sometimes at as high as a 10 percent rate. By buying cheap and selling dear, she helped Wang earn high interest and become increasingly wealthy. Because Zhai haggled over every penny, her own savings also exceeded a thousand strings of cash coins. She secretly exchanged her cash coins for gold and silver.

Zhai had no family or relatives. At almost forty, her only wish was to make plans for the rest of her life. Wang was a shrewd and deceitful merchant. Although he considered Zhai ugly and vulgar, he was attracted by her wealth. Wang tempted Zhai with the prospect of becoming his wife. As a result, Zhai entrusted all her savings to Wang.

One day, Wang and Zhai were about to cross the [Yangzi] River. The night before, they had stayed at an inn. Wang got up before dawn, loaded the boat with all the luggage, and quickly unfastened the mooring rope. By the time Zhai reached the water bank, the boat was already far away. Zhai grieved for a few hours. Seeing no hope in life, she threw herself into the water and drowned.

Wang witnessed this from afar. [Seeing that Zhai had died,] Wang thought that he had succeeded in seizing all of Zhai's property. He then returned to his hometown to manage his livelihood and built a residence to settle in. Soon enough, he led an even more luxurious life than he had before.

Wang had two young sons. Both were sharp and clever. One day, when they were playing near the house, a servant of the family, who had been resentful of the boys' father, took a knife and killed the two boys. Ever since that day, strange things would happen in the family. Some saw a woman with an extraordinary body, who looked like Zhai, leading a legion of ghosts and howling monsters. They would either hit a drum or strike metal at midnight, manifesting in thousands of different forms and shapes. They would move tables, cases, and vessels from inside the house and arrange them in the yard. Wang's eldest son was furious and ordered exorcists to eliminate the ghosts and monsters, but the beings did not stop. The son acted in a more unrestrained manner, even to the point of slandering and demeaning Heaven.

Later, for beating people to death while drunk, he was spared his life, but was tattooed and exiled to Lingnan.[34]

[Following the eldest son's banishment,] Wang's second son became the only one left in the household, but he had troublemakers as close friends. He would have arguments with them after getting drunk and was eventually murdered. In the end, Wang died distressed and dispirited. His wife died of poverty and starvation. No one gave her a burial, so her body remained exposed. The Wangs' house went to others in the same clan. (*YJZ, zhiyi*:1.802–3)

76 • The Tea Shop Servant Cui San

Li Shiliu, a resident of Huangzhou [Huanggang, Hubei], opened a tea shop under the Guanfeng Bridge. On a spring night in the eighth year of the Chunxi reign period [1181], the shop was already closed. Li's servant, Cui San, was not yet asleep when he heard someone knocking at the door. Cui asked who it was. The person outside answered, "It is me." Cui thought it was his master, so he quickly opened the door.

Outside stood a very beautiful young woman. Shocked at the sight of the stranger, Cui inquired, "Where are you from? This is Li's Tea Shop. Have you come to the wrong place?" The woman answered, "I am the daughter-in-law of the Sun family to the left of your shop. Because I angered my mother-in-law, I was chased out of the house. I did not have anywhere to go for the night and would request that you allow me to stay overnight here." Cui said, "I am a hired laborer. How could I give you permission without authorization?" The woman entreated and threatened to kill herself if Cui did not let her in; she sobbed and would not leave.

Hesitantly, Cui led the woman to a corner on one side of the tea shop and gave her a mat to sleep on. A long while later, she got up to approach

---

34. Lingnan, literally, "south of the Ridges," refers to the large region south of the Dayu, Qitian, Dupang, Mengzhu, and Yuecheng Ridges, generally referring to modern Guangdong, Guangxi, and Hainan Provinces. In the Song, Lingnan was a destination for political exiles and ordinary criminals.

Cui's bed, speaking to him in an intimate voice, "I am not used to sleeping alone. Are you interested in sharing a bed?" Cui was overjoyed with the proposal, so kept her with him. Cui and the woman slept together. She left when the rooster crowed.

From then on, the woman would occasionally come to visit Cui San. As a servant, Cui was pleased that he could have such a good woman to keep him company. She satisfied all his wishes. For this reason, Cui San was never suspicious of the entire incident.

One night, the woman said, "Your monthly compensation does not exceed a thousand cash coins. It would not be enough to cover your expenses." She took out paper money that was worth ten thousand cash coins and gave it to Cui. From then on, she would frequently aid him in small amounts. Cui was even more pleased.

Cui San's older brother, Cui Er, was a good hunter and often traveled to other prefectures. One day, Cui Er stopped by at his younger brother's, but ended up staying for more than ten days. The woman stopped coming during this time. Cui San missed her terribly, so much so that he dreamed about her. He then told Cui Er his secret. Cui Er said, "This place is replete with ghosts and monsters. I worry that she might hurt you. We should make a plan immediately [to find out if she is human]." Cui San said, "I have associated with her for half a year and relied on her to support me. Our relationship is as righteous as that of husband and wife. It is unreasonable to suspect her to be a ghost." The older brother said, "But knowing that I am here, she has disappeared completely. Why is this?" Cui San answered, "It is probably because we are brothers. The rites prohibit a sister-in-law and a brother-in-law from staying in close quarters." The older brother asked, "When she comes, where does she come in and get out?" Cui San said, "She enters through the outer door and comes down from the stairs."

That night, the older brother pretended to have left, taking his hunting weapons and spreading out several nets around the house. At dusk, he hid in a covered place. After midnight, there were suddenly noises. Cui Er rushed to light a campfire to see what was caught in the net. It was a spotted fox, three *chi* [about one meter or three feet] in length and already dead. The older brother said, "This is what has been captivating you." He then skinned the fox and boiled its meat. With tears in his eyes, Cui San felt miserable and dejected. [Even after knowing she was a fox spirit,] he could not overcome his feelings for her.

Another day, when Cui San was in the room alone, he smelled an extraordinarily strong fragrance. The woman was already standing under the lamp, cursing him loudly, "You and I loved each other so, and I aided you when you were experiencing hardships. Why did you so easily believe your arrogant older brother's words? Fortunately, I had not left the house at the time. He only killed a maid and damaged a jacket." Cui apologized and thanked the woman. The woman smiled and said, "I knew you did not do it. I do not hate you." She then stayed at Cui's as before. She is still around. *Zhu Conglong told this and the previous stories.* (*YJZ, zhiyi:*2.805–6)

77 • The Tomb Land of Old Jiao

Thirty *li* [about fifteen kilometers or ten miles] outside of the Western Gate of Fangzhou [Fangxian, Hubei], there was a stone cliff that was extremely precipitous. Below the cliff, there was a stone room. Next to it was a Daoist shrine named the Nine-Room Palace. People say that, when Chen Xiyi lived a reclusive life in Mount Hua, he also stayed in this place.[35] The stone room was his bedroom. At the time, there was an old man Jiao who lived at the foot of the mountain. Chen would visit Jiao every day. When Chen was about to arrive, two cranes would hover and glide in the air before they landed while dancing. Jiao would wait for Chen based on this sign. He would have his entire family come out to greet Chen and prepare tea and fruit to entertain him. It went on like this for a year.

One day, Chen told Jiao that he was leaving. Jiao inquired, "Where are you going?" Chen answered, "I want to go back to the Three Peaks [at Mount Hua]." Jiao and his son insisted that Chen stay longer, to no avail. Chen then asked Jiao, "What would your family wish for? Would you want official ranking? Wealth?" Jiao said, "We live in poor mountains and are ignorant people, so do not wish to serve the government. If the family could

---

35. Chen Xiyi was a famous Daoist in the tenth century. Mount Hua, located in modern Shaanxi Province, is the West Peak of the famous Five Peaks. The other four peaks are Mount Tai in Shandong, Mount Heng in Shanxi, Mount Song in Henan, and Mount Heng in Hunan.

possess a thousand head of oxen, it would complete my aspirations." Chen smiled and said, "This is easy." He took Jiao with him into the mountains. Pointing to a cave, Chen said, "Have yourself buried here when you die, and you will realize your wish." He then bid his farewell.

When Old Jiao died, his son carried his coffin and had him buried in the cave that Chen had identified. In several years, the family's wealth and estate were abundant. The number of farming oxen they owned surely reached a thousand head. It has been two hundred years since then, and Jiao's descendants still keep their old estate. Although the number of oxen that they owned has decreased compared to the original thousand, the Jiaos are still among the richest in the village. Villagers called the place where Jiao was buried the Tomb Land of Old Jiao. *Zhang Qi (courtesy name Ziwen) told this and the previous stories.* (*YJZ, zhiyi*:4.825–26)

78 • The Attendant of Monk Yongwu

Yongwu, a monk of Fuzhou, often visited Buddhist monasteries. Everywhere he stayed, he would bring his nephew as his attendant. Yongwu was harsh and strict about following religious rules. Whoever broke a rule would surely be punished. His nephew's excessive behavior, however, was always given preferential treatment. Yongwu never criticized the nephew, not even slightly. No one dared to say anything about it.

Later when Yongwu lived at the Guoqing Temple in Taizhou [in Zhejiang], his nephew had become even more unrestrained. Those in high positions at the temple all turned against him. They went to the chief abbot and said, "If he is not ousted, many of us are going to leave." It was not until then that Yongwu said sadly, "I could not bear to bring this up in the past. I know now that I cannot hide the truth anymore. This monk [i.e., the nephew] was actually my mother." Everyone bowed and asked him to explain. Yongwu said, "Although I had become a monk, I used to sit in meditation at my old house. At the time, my mother had just passed away. One night, I saw her entering my older brother's house with her face covered. I was shocked to see her and was about to get up to follow her when I heard my pregnant sister-in-law giving birth to a boy [at the exact moment of my mother's appearance]. [Knowing that my nephew was the reincarnation of my mother,] when he grew up, I purchased him an ordination certificate and had his hair shaved [in order to become a monk]. This way, I could have him follow me. For this reason, even though I knew he often violated monastery rules, I could not bring myself to discipline him."

Everyone sighed and regretted that they had brought this matter up. They thanked Yongwu for telling them the truth. Yongwu said, "Now that the matter is exposed, he is not suitable to stay here any longer." He then had the nephew ousted from the monastery. Not long after, Yongwu also left his position, leaving for Nankang [Ganzhou, Jiangxi] with his nephew. *The Elder of Doushuai, Faduan, told this story when I saw him.* (*YJZ, zhiyi*:6.842)

79 • An Official from Yixing

In the spring of the fifth year of the Shaoxing reign period [1135], an official from Yixing [in Jiangsu], Wu Guan, suffered from a very serious eye problem. [Taking his ailment as an inauspicious sign,] he brought his wife and children to Yuhang [in Zhejiang], hoping the trip would allow him to avoid calamities. Wu once served in this county and had purchased a small residence as a temporary lodging place when he traveled. This time, the entire family moved into it.

Over a month later, Wu suddenly wished to go home. His wife wanted to stay for a little longer because she had sent someone to Lin'an [Hangzhou, Zhejiang] to make purchases and wanted to wait for his return. Wu was adamant that this would not do, as if someone were pressuring him to leave. He left only one servant to look after the house before heading to the road and did not even bid farewell to friends.

The next evening, the area around Mount Tianmu flooded. River water suddenly rushed over the land. It was several feet deep on level ground. Wu's house was submerged in water, and the servant drowned. At the time, people who suffered from the catastrophe numbered over a hundred thousand. (*YJZ, zhiyi*:8.858)

80 • Wang Wugong's Wife

Wang Wugong of the capital lived in the Jiyou Lane and had a beautiful wife. Once, an alms-begging monk passed by Wang's door. Catching sight of Wang's wife, the monk became infatuated with her. He secretly made plans to flirt with and seduce the woman, but did not get a chance to do so [when he heard that] Wang Wugong was about to assume a position in the Huai region.

One day before their departure from the capital, Wang and his wife were sitting behind a screen when a servant came with a box. Placing the box in front of Wang's wife, the servant said, "Master Cong [i.e., the monk] has a message for your lady. It's been sometime since the two of you last saw each other. There is nothing to express his affection for you. He simply wanted to present this as a farewell gift." After saying these words, the servant left the Wangs.

The couple rushed to open the box and found a hundred jade seals in it. Opening one of the seals, they found a tiny gold tablet hidden, which weighed one *qian* [about 3.7 grams or 0.13 ounces]. At first, they thought that the tablet might have been mistakenly placed there. Upon opening others, they found that all contained the same gold piece. Furious, Wang scolded his wife, "I had suspected that something was not right when the bald one [i.e., the monk] passed by our gate day and night. Now it is proven to be true [that you two have been having an illicit affair]." Wang then brought a lawsuit to the prefectural authorities against the monk and his wife for adultery.

No one knew the monk's name or his place of residence. He had since fled and was nowhere to be found. Wang's wife was imprisoned and interrogated, but the only thing she did after her arrest was wailing and lamenting to Heaven [the injustice that had befallen her]. She could not answer a single question by the authorities either. At the same time, Wang left her behind and went to assume his position by himself.

Wang's wife was imprisoned for several months. Because the accusation against her was ambiguous, a verdict could not be reached. The prefect subsequently ordered that she be registered as a criminal and placed under house arrest. The woman was unable to support herself, to the extent that she had nothing to eat.

When the monk heard about the woman's situation, he snuck back into town and secretly sent a sewing lady to persuade Wang's wife. The sewing lady said, "What are you going to do now? You will starve to death. I can take you to a temple, where you can support yourself by doing needlework while you wait for your husband to change his mind. What do you think?" Wang's wife followed this advice hesitantly.

When Wang's wife arrived at the temple, she was led right into the monk's room. The monk hid her in a cellar, raping and humiliating her as he pleased. As time passed, he began to allow her some freedom to come and go. The woman eventually found an opportunity to inform the patrolling soldiers of her circumstances. The monk was captured and punished for the crime he had committed. Wang's wife died soon after from bitterness and resentment. (*YJZ, zhijing*:3.902)

81 • The Grave of Vice Director Rong

Vice Director Rong Maoshi (given name Ni) was buried to the southwest of Mount Bian in Huzhou [in Zhejiang]. Ten years after he was laid to rest, the Daoist Xu Cunzhen came to the burial place and said to the monk at the family temple, "This was originally a fine plot for burial. Recently, the good energy around here has disappeared completely. The decline of the family will occur in the next two to three years. If the family immediately divines for another burial ground and moves the graves there, it might be able to save half its fortune. If they procrastinate and do nothing, disaster will be inevitable."

The monk told Rong's son, Jian, what he had heard, but Jian did not pay much attention to the advice. This was the case [partially] because the matter was of great significance and could not be managed in a short time. Jian died shortly thereafter. This was followed by his sons, assistant magistrate of Qianshan [in Jiangxi], Fuchen, Administrator for Public Order of Nankang [in Jiangxi], Yingchen, and magistrate of Renhe [in Zhejiang], Shouchen. Seventeen women in the family also died in the next few years. Now only one grandson, assistant magistrate of Taoyuan [in Hunan], Gongchen, is alive. The importance of the location of one's family graves amounts to such! How could this be a coincidence? Cunzhen was indeed an extraordinary person. (*YJZ, zhijing*:4.912)

82 • The Butcher Tong Qi

Thirty *li* [about fifteen kilometers or ten miles] from Taizhou [in Zhejiang] was a small temple called Jingshan. At the intersection nearby, there was a butcher, Tong Qi [Qi means Seven]. For generations, Tong's family had been in the trade of slaughtering pigs. Every year, he would kill over a thousand head. He also peddled meat in the city, using the income to enrich his family.

On the New Year's Eve of the first year of the Chunxi reign period [1174], someone in the family dreamt about all the ancestors from their father's and grandfather's generations gathering together. The ancestors said, "Because Little Seven did not change the family's old profession, we have all been reincarnated into pigs more than ten times and have died at his hand. What you keep in the pigsty are all reincarnations of your ancestors, but we have already repaid our debt. Be sure not to kill any more pigs."

The next day, the person who had the dream went to the pigsty and saw all the pigs there having human heads that resembled those of his ancestors. Everyone spoke to him while looking sad and distressed. What they said was similar to the content of the previous night's dream. Their lower bodies, however, remained those of pigs. In a short while, everything returned to normal. Nonfamily members would see nothing out of the ordinary.

[After hearing what had happened,] Tong immediately emptied all the pigsties, donating all the pigs to the Buddhist temple. He also offered meals to the monks and repented to the Buddha. From then on, Tong took pains to reform himself and demonstrate his regrets [for killing animals]. He changed his profession to peddling yarns and silk to support his family. He is still alive. (*YJZ, zhijing*:5.916–17)

83 • Rujiao's Deer Mother

Rujiao was a monk at the family temple of the Lis, a rich household in Gucheng, located in Lin'an in Taizhou [in Zhejiang]. His mother, Lady Ye, lived in a village north of town with his eldest brother. Rujiao often went to visit her. In the spring of the thirteenth year of the Chunxi reign period [1186], his mother passed away. On the first anniversary of her death, after preparing a sacrificial service, Rujiao returned to the temple to continue to mourn his mother.

One day, he dreamt about his mother visiting him. Lowering her head and weeping, she said, "Because I did not do good deeds my whole life, I have been reincarnated into a deer. I live in the nearby mountains. Tomorrow morning, I will be chased by eagles and hunting dogs. You can go and look. If you see me, you can redeem me with money. Be sure not to forget." Rujiao woke up and was saddened by the dream.

As soon as it became light, Rujiao led several servants waiting outside of the temple. Surely enough, between the *chen* [7 a.m. to 9 a.m.] and *si* [9 a.m. to 11 a.m.] hours, there appeared hunters chasing a deer. The deer ran straight into the temple. Rujiao gave five thousand cash coins to the hunters in exchange for the deer. He then kept and raised the deer himself.

Three years later, Rujiao dreamt about his mother again. In the dream, his mother said, "I have repaid my karma and was spared the fate of feeding humans with my body. This was all due to your filial sentiments." When Rujiao got up in the morning, the deer was already dead in the enclosure. Rujiao buried its body on the side of his mother's grave. Villagers called it the Tomb of the Deer Mother. (*YJZ, zhiding*:3.984)

84 • Runner at the Raofeng Postal Station

Between Jin [Ankang, Shaanxi] and Yang [Xixiang, Shaanxi], the postal road was desolate, but there was a station every ten *li* [about 5 kilometers or 3.3 miles].[36] One day, a runner at the Raofeng Postal Station was on his way to deliver a document. When it was getting dark, he ran into a tiger, who intended to maul and eat him. Extremely hard pressed, the runner stood still and talked to the tiger, "I heard that tigers are intelligent animals. The document that I am delivering is a confidential order from the court to the Military Commissioner. There is nothing I can do if you eat me. But what will happen to the imperial order if the contents of this bag are not delivered?" The tiger lowered its head and listened attentively. It then left immediately.

After delivering the document at the next postal station, the runner stayed overnight, where he told people about his encounter with the tiger and was pleased that he got a second life. The next day, when he returned to where the tiger had been, he ran into the animal again and was eaten. This story shows that the runner was destined to be killed by a tiger. His escape from the first encounter must have been due to the importance of the official document. *Someone at the postal station related this and the previous two stories.* (*YJZ, zhijing*:5.1006–7)

85 • Ah Xu Going to the Underworld

Ah Xu, wife of Wang San of Fengxian Village in Jiaxing [in Zhejiang], died in the early summer of the first year of the Qiandao reign period [1165]. She came back to life overnight and recounted to people her experience, "I

---

36. The Song government maintained a network of thousands of lodging and postal stations throughout the country for transportation and communication purposes. These facilities were distributed along the official roads and waterways that connected the capital with remote places of the empire. Each station was equipped with, among other things, horses and soldiers.

was very ill when I saw two government runners. Holding official documents
in their hands, they chased after me and said, 'We are here to call you to confirm something at the court.' I responded by saying, 'My husband and son
are the ones who manage everyday household matters. I am never involved
in such things. Why are you chasing me instead?' The runners answered, 'We
need you to go with us.' Before I realized it, I had followed them out of the
door and onto a path. It was cloudy and gloomy. I could not see clearly. After
walking over ten *li* [about 5 kilometers or 3.3 miles], we arrived at the government office. People came and went in a hurry, making much noise. The
runners stopped me outside and entered to report that they had escorted me
here. They then ordered me to a hall. There were curtains on four sides of
it. A clerk who stood in the front asked, 'Why did you seize the properties
of the weak and the young?' I said, 'I do not normally intervene in family
matters. I have been a vegetarian and have chanted the name of the Buddha
for over thirty years. The only thing I can remember [that might be relevant
to what you are inquiring] is that my elder brother-in-law, Wang Da, and my
husband, Wang San, divided the family estate into two equal shares. Brother-
in-law later left home to become a Buddhist novice at the Dasheng Monastery. His share of the estate was mortgaged by his son, Wang Ba, to the
Sun family in Weitang Township. Wang Ba used the money on gambling and
never spent it sensibly. As a result, the only thing left of his share of the family property was the foundation to the house, which I rented. Brother-in-law
died many years later. Since Wang Ba had left home and not returned at the
time of his father's death, my husband Wang San had his older brother cremated and the ashes dispersed. We later returned the foundation to Wang Ba
for him to build a house. Except for that, we never forcefully took anything
from the nephew.' I then heard a voice from behind the curtain, 'Have Wang
Da escorted out to confront Ah Xu.' Immediately, there stood a criminal in
a cangue below the stairs. It was Brother-in-law. He turned to me and said, 'I
had been in the underworld for a long time and did not know exactly what
had happened in the world of the living. This was why I brought lawsuits
against you twice, [thinking that you had misappropriated my and my son's
estate]. Now that everything is clear, I am no longer willing to fight.' I asked,
'Why are you suffering like this?' Brother-in-law said, 'When I was a Buddhist novice, I was charged with begging alms from patrons for the purpose
of building a bell tower for the monastery, but I hid and kept the money

that I begged for myself. I also brought home the food given to monks by donors. For this reason, I have not been spared from torture.' With the confrontation over, I begged to be released. The person behind the curtains said, 'How could we allow a person who has visited here to leave without suffering anything?' They then forced me to sit down and beat my back. By the third lash, as if waking up from a dream, I suddenly returned to life."

Ah Xu's family looked at her back. The whip marks were still there and were causing extreme pain. The scars took days to heal. Sun Qi, the new magistrate of Guangde, who was from the same county as Ah Xu, wrote this story down. *Yu Weisi told this and the three previous stories.* (*YJZ, zhijing*:6.1013–14)

86 • The Marital Relations of the Dings and Lus

Ding Liuweng of Dexing [in Jiangxi] was related by marriage to Lu Erweng of the same county. Their residences were separated by a large town. Both families were devoted to farming and sericulture and were upper households.[37] Lu's younger brother had been wandering in other regions. When he returned more than twenty years later, he asked Lu Erweng to divide the family property. Lu was stingy in the process, so the younger brother brought a lawsuit to the county. Before the court intervened, Lu Erweng gathered all the family's gold, silk, and other movable properties, entrusting them to Ding Liuweng. In the subsequent court-ordered property division, the Lus' land and gardens, which were recorded in contracts and certificates, were divided into two equal halves between Lu Erweng and his younger brother. Only then did the dispute end.

A short while after the lawsuit was settled, Lu Erweng visited Ding Liuweng, asking him to return what he had hidden at the Dings. Ding said,

---

37. In the Song, all rural households were categorized into five grades based on the value of their estate and the taxes they paid. The top three grades were called upper households, the fourth and fifth grades lower households. Here the author simply implied that both families were wealthy.

"The litigation between you and your brother has just ended and you suddenly take these things home. Should it become known, you would be causing a disaster for yourself. I too would be harassed by the authorities, who might pressure me to testify to your crime. It is possible that I might even be implicated and found guilty. It might be better to leave the items at my house for a bit longer. It would make sense for you to take some home over time." Lu was pleased by Ding's words and thanked him, believing what Ding said to be his honest thoughts.

Two years after their conversation, Lu asked Ding again. This time, Ding denied profusely and said, "You must be joking! How could it be possible that you entrusted such a large amount of wealth to me without having even one written word or a shred of paper as proof? Why do you not go to reason with the authorities?" Lu realized that Ding had the intention of misappropriating his properties. But knowing that he could not expose his previous scheme to incur a lawsuit from his younger brother, Lu endured misery and died despondently.

[Upon hearing of Lu's death,] Ding went to make offerings to Lu's spirit and wept there. He also extended his condolences to Lu's sons. When Ding returned home, he saw old man Lu sitting in the hall. Seeing Ding, Lu greeted him. The two exchanged polite pleasantries. Ding then said, "You are already dead. Why are you here?" Lu replied, "Because you misappropriated the properties that I temporarily left with you, I died with a grievance in my heart. I have come to take my wealth back. You should give them back to my sons. Otherwise, I will never leave you alone." Ding answered, "Your body is on the way to the underworld. What would you need property for? How about I gather many monks and have them recite Buddhist scriptures? This will accumulate more karma to aid in your fortune in the next life." Lu did not agree. After he and Ding argued back and forth with each other for some time, Lu got up angrily and said, "I am leaving. You make up your mind." He then disappeared. Ding knew in his heart that what he had done was not righteous, but unable to change his greedy nature, he was not willing to give the wealth back to Lu's sons in the end.

Several months later, Lu came again during the day and cursed Ding furiously, "I died because of you and have not held you responsible for it. I have only asked you to return the properties that I entrusted to you. I have tried everything to help you see that what you did was wrong, yet you have shown no sign of repentance. Let us verify everything in the underworld."

Ding's sons and brothers who were present all heard what Lu said. A short while later, Lu grasped Ding, who then fell to the ground and died. Ding's family helped him up and tried to resurrect him, but it was too late. *Bao Qiyun, a scholar in the county, told this story.* (*YJZ, zhigeng*:1.1137–38)

87 • Director Wu Zhongquan

In the early years of the Chunxi reign period [1174–1189], Dong Juhou (courtesy name Chunfu) of Linchuan [in Jiangxi] came to the capital for a reassignment after having completed his tenure as the professor of Jingzhou. Before he was appointed to a new position, he fell ill and died at an inn with no relatives or friends at his side. At the time, Wu Zhongquan (courtesy name Yi) of Chongren [in Jiangxi] was a proofreader in the Palace Library. He and Dong had not been very close, but because they were from the same prefecture, Wu managed Dong's medical treatment, prepared him a coffin when he died, mailed his belongings home, and sent a messenger to notify Dong's family of his passing all by himself.

In the second year of the Qingyuan reign [1196], Wu, at the rank of Secretarial Court Gentleman, was appointed to a position in charge of fiscal affairs in Hunan. In the fourth month of the next year, he was transferred to Guangxi and was soon censured and dismissed. Wu then returned home and began building a large residence. Because he drank so much and was always intoxicated, he completely stopped eating. As a result, Wu became as thin as a piece of standing firewood, but his astuteness did not decline whatsoever.

By winter Wu fell ill, feeling heavy and drowsy. Suddenly, he called his family to prepare tea and hot water, saying, "Professor Dong is coming to see me." His family wondered and asked who Dong was. Wu answered, "His name is Chunfu." In a short while, people saw Wu nodding and responding, as if he was talking to someone. He acted the same the next day, as if he was constantly talking to a person. When people inquired where the person was, he would point his walking stick and say, "He is sitting right there. He told me that I will pass away at noon the day after tomorrow. You can cook a vegetarian meal to send him off first."

By this time, Wu's family knew that he was dealing with a ghost. All were worried and terrified. The next day, Wu requested a bath. After arranging the bathtub in the room, the maid enclosed it with a screen. Wu asked, "What for?" The maid answered, "I was afraid that you might be affected by a draft." Wu laughed, "How could I be afraid of wind at this point?"

After the bath, Wu put on his clothes and cap. The maid helped him into the hall room in the back, where he bid his farewell at the family shrine. Coming out of the shrine, Wu ordered that wine be prepared. As he drank, he said goodbye to his wife, sons, and nephews. He also asked his concubines to sing *ci* lyrics, even harmonizing with them. After drinking for five rounds, Wu ended the banquet. He then wrote his will. The first item listed in the document was that his family not abandon the clan's charitable school. The second concerned managing family affairs. The last instruction directed that all his concubines be married off. In this way, Wu arranged all family matters in an orderly and clear manner. However, every time he wrote the name of a concubine, he looked saddened and greatly pained.

Altogether, Wu used several pieces of paper to complete his will. [When all was finished,] he put down the ink brush and fell into a lethargic sleep. When Wu woke up, he acted as if he had seen Dong coming to get him and chided Dong, "Chunfu, you go first. Do not bother us." Wu then ordered his hair done and tossed and turned the entire night. He later ordered a servant to give him the time. Surely enough, Wu died at noon. He was not even sixty. It is a shame. (*YJZ, sanzhi:ren*:1.1468–69)

88 • Gourd-Shaped Dates

Outside the entrance to an old lady's house, seven *li* [about 3.5 kilometers or about 2 miles] outside of Guangzhou [in Henan], there grew two date trees. One day in the fall when the dates were ripe, a Daoist passed by and asked for some dates from the old lady. She responded, "My son is away in the fields. No one can strike them down for you. I would not mind [if you did it yourself]. You can eat as many as you want." The Daoist picked and ate about a dozen dates. He then tied a gourd that he wore on the tip of a twig. Before leaving, he turned to the old lady and said, "Thank you for your generosity. Next year, this tree will grow dates in the shape of this gourd. Since it is a new variety, you will make three times as much money." The Daoist left after these words.

Next year, the tree indeed grew gourd-shaped dates, just as the Daoist said. Nowadays there is still this variety in Guangzhou. Although people had taken the pits and planted them elsewhere, the trees would not grow the same kind of dates. (*YJZ, sanzhi:ren*:6.1509)

89 • Kui Boshan

Kui Shisan (courtesy name Boshan) was a resident of Raozhou [in Jiangxi]. In the early years of the Chunxi reign period [1174–1189], he joined the family of Wang Xiaosan near the Binzhou Gate as a married-in son-in-law. In his daily conduct, Kui lacked wit and thoughtfulness. He was used to sitting idly and waiting for food to be served to him. The Wangs could not stand Kui. They often forced Kui out of the house, not allowing him to see his wife. Kui humbly implored his wife's parents many times, but they would not listen. They went so far as having their daughter divorce Kui.

At the end of his rope, Kui had nothing on which to support himself. In the winter of the twelfth year of the Chunxi reign period [1185], he killed himself with a knife outside his wife's residence. The son of Xiaosan's elder brother, Xiaoqi, a clerk at the prefecture, fumed at what Kui had done. He instigated his uncle [i.e., Kui's father-in-law] to present his side of the story to the authorities, requesting for a thorough investigation. This was intended to prevent vicious young men from the Kui family holding the Wangs hostage in the future.

Ever since the official investigation, members of the Kuis would appear day and night, harassing the Wangs. None of the Wangs would dare to pass by the Kuis' entrance. Everyone was fearful of them.

Three years later, on the first day of the first month, Xiaoqi suffered from a hangover. His wife went into the kitchen to make soup to dispel the effects of alcohol. When she was about to come back into the room where her husband was, she saw him shouting in bed while beating the mat. He had spat so much that his spit soaked the quilt. Xiaoqi died instantly; by the time his wife came back to the room, it was already too late to save him. People thought that Xiaoqi must have been haunted to death by Kui. (*YJZ, sanzhi:ren*:6.1513)

90 • Two Epitaphs for the Lis

Anxing, the son of my fellow native, Li Wenzhong, earned the examination degree and served as the assistant magistrate in Dehua County in Jiangzhou [Jiujiang, Jiangxi]. Anxing brought his father to his office, where Wenzhong died in the first month of the fourth year in the Shaoxi reign period [1193]. The year Anxing passed the examination at the Department of Ritual, I oversaw the examinations. Based on this connection, he came to ask me for an epitaph for his father. I composed one at his request. Kangshi, Anxing's uncle, saw the epitaph and sighed with admiration. He then said to his son, Zhongxing, "When I die, could I have an epitaph like this one?" Two months and two years later, Kangshi passed away. Zhongxing and his older brother, Yingxing, recollecting their father's wish, came to make a request, which I could not bear to decline.

[Right at the time when I was finishing up the epitaph,] Miss Wu, Yingxing's wife, was napping when she dreamt about Wenzhong and Kangshi sitting in the hall. Both excited, they laughed heartily and said to each other, "We now have the writing of *neihan* [the Grand Councilor in the Palace; i.e., Hong Mai]." Miss Wu had just awoken when she heard servants reporting from outside that *neihan* had had someone deliver the epitaph to the house. In the first month of the fourth year of the Qingyuan reign period [1198], Zhongxing came to the prefecture and told this to Huang Shang. He also recorded the episode to show it to me. (*YJZ, sanzhi:ren*:7.1522–23)

91 • Petty Clerk Xie

Xie, a petty clerk at Nancheng County [Mengjin, Henan], was extremely filial to his father. His father was old and needed wine and meat for sustenance. The clerk's family was poor, but if he estimated that there was enough to cover a day's expenses, he would not lack in providing for his father. If there was even a small amount to spare, he would buy nice food to present to his father. He did not dare to do anything excessive, however, in case his father would worry about the family's finances. For twenty years, he showed no variance in his actions.

When the father was dying, he held Xie's hand and sobbed, saying, "You have done your best to be filial to me. Deities and Heaven have all borne witness. I have nothing to repay you. When I die, I am willing to be your son."

At the time, Xie's wife was pregnant. When she was about to give birth, she dreamt that her father-in-law entered her room. When she woke up from her dream, she gave birth to a son, whose appearance resembled that of her in-law. When the son was several years old, whenever the family offered sacrifices to the ancestors, he would occupy the position of his grandfather, eating and drinking freely. When he grew up, he treated his parents in the same manner as Xie had. (*YJZ, bu*:1.1553)

92 • Old Woman Chen's Dog

In the third month of the fourteenth year of the Chunxi reign period [1187], Zhao Er of Jiangzhou [Jiujiang, Jiangxi] left the market and passed by the South Gate. A dog at Old Woman Chen's came to greet him, wagging its tail and prostrating itself. Zhao was surprised and said, "I have never been here before and you do not know me. Why are you acting so strangely?" The dog suddenly spoke in human language, "I was your close friend [in a previous life]. At the time that we knew each other, I was Little Wulang of the teashop at the market. I should not have called my mother 'old bitch' frequently in my previous life. For this I was punished and reincarnated as an animal. The reason I am telling you this myself is so that people of the world can use me as a warning." Zhao sighed. When he wanted to speak more, the dog barked and ran away. (*YJZ, bu*:1.1557)

93 • Chaste Woman Cheng

After Fang La [1048–1121] started a rebellion, he led the bandits to Xin'an [Chun'an, Zhejiang]. The family of Cheng Shuqing of She [in Anhui] took refuge to the south of the town. The couple had a daughter, who was seventeen years old, and they deliberated [about what might befall her if she was captured by the rebels]: "This is our home. We will die if misfortune occurs, but our daughter is in her prime both in terms of her age and her appearance. If she is disgraced by the rebels, how can we bear to face our clansmen?" So, they called their daughter over and said, "Our prefecture considers licentiousness a disgrace. You are the daughter of a good family. You do not normally step beyond the gate of the residence. If you are coerced by the rebels, what would you do?" The daughter answered, "Is your daughter the kind of woman who would submit to the rebels? If something terrible happens, my only option is to die." She then picked up their clothes, pretending to carry them while walking fast, then acted out the scenes in which she was seized and tried to resist the bandits. Her parents were pleased and said, "If you could behave in this manner, you are truly the daughter we have raised you to be."

The next day, the rebels came. The Chengs fled and were separated in the mountains. The daughter happened to run into the rebels and was caught. A rebel said, "I will take you back to His Sagaciousness [i.e., Fang La]. Why would I need to worry about not having wealth and power?" The girl cursed, "You dogs deceive Heaven and harm the people. You are not even on a par with birds and beasts, not to mention a sagacious person!" The rebel threatened her with a bared blade and said, "If you do not obey, I will kill you." The girl cursed even more. The bandit was enraged. He first cut her hair bun.

Seeing that she could not be subdued, he killed her and cut her body into parts and left.

At the time when this happened, two boys were hiding behind a large boulder and saw the entire incident. They went home and told their families, who buried the Chengs' daughter at the foot of the mountain. Luo Song (courtesy name Duanshi) wrote a biography for her. (*YJZ, bu*:1.1557)

94 • Wenren Banghua

The Wenren family in Guixi of Xinzhou [Shangrao, Jiangxi] had two sons. The elder one's name was Bangrong and the younger one Banghua. When their father was alive, he made plans for the sons' livelihood in advance. The father opened a tea shop in the county seat to give it to Banghua and a pharmacy in the prefectural seat for Bangrong. In the years following the death of their father, Banghua was indulgent and wasteful. He almost ruined his business completely. Bangrong, on the other hand, established himself and was frugal in his expenditures, and so lived a life of plenty. Their mother favored the younger son. Not only did she secretly help Banghua, she also influenced him into bringing a lawsuit against his older brother, alleging that, while the mother was still alive, the family property should not have been divided.[38]

Bangrong refused to comply with the official verdict, which favored the younger brother, and appealed to the higher authorities. Officials at the Censorate and the Prefecture deliberated the case five or six times without being able to reach a consensus. Eventually it was the son of Zhang Zhen, Commissioner of the Armory, who adjudicated the case. By this time, the mother had passed away. Zhang ordered that all remaining funds of the Wenren

---

38. The mother had a point regarding the family division issue, which was clearly stipulated in the *Song Penal Code*. In real-life scenarios, such as the one presented here, many families, out of a variety of considerations, did go through property divisions while one or both parents were still alive. In adjudicating individual cases, the local judges also demonstrated much flexibility. As the next sentence implied, the judge did rule in favor of the mother and the younger brother.

family be registered. Each brother received a certain amount. The property ruined earlier by Banghua was to be counted toward his share. Banghua refused to accept the verdict. Both brothers were subsequently put in prison.

[From prison,] Banghua had a friend buy some raw arsenic and put it in a bowl of soup, then bribed a prison guard to pass the soup to Bangrong. Bangrong received the soup and ate it. As soon as he had swallowed some, he began to vomit and his body turned red and swollen. The guard quickly informed the judicial official of the incident, who sent Bangrong home to recover. He nevertheless died half a day later.

Lianfu, Bangrong's son, knew Bangrong had been poisoned, but he had no proof with which to redress the injustice, so had his father buried, all the while enduring insults and humiliations. [Even though Lianfu did not have hard evidence about his father's murder, he eventually brought Banghua to court.] A year after the incident, Banghua was called to the judicial office to answer the charge from Lianfu against him and was put in prison. A servant of Lianfu suggested that they adopt the strategy used earlier by Banghua; Lianfu and the servant brought another person to a food shop with them, where the three men bought four bowls of noodles. They each had one bowl and left the last one for Banghua. Before sending it to him, they minced arsenic and put it in the noodles. [When the noodle was delivered to him,] Banghua did not finish the entire bowl. The prisoner next to him, who was awaiting capital punishment, had the rest, but threw some soup on the ground. A dog licked the soup from the ground. In a short while, both the prisoner and the dog began to vomit. Banghua also became sick. His symptoms were the same as those of his brother. He died the next morning.

The administrator for judicial affairs, Wang Changzu, became deeply suspicious of Banghua's death. Wang said, "Yesterday, Banghua was a strong man with no illness. How could he suddenly die?" Wang immediately started an investigation of the cause of Banghua's death. He sent out prison guards to find the noodle shop, where they learned from the owner that three people had come to eat there the previous day. One wore a black jacket, the other two had on white outerwear. Wang rushed to send prison guards for the men's arrest, but all three had fled. [They did determine that] the one wearing black was Lianfu and the two wearing white were Lianfu's servants. Wang informed these findings to the prefect, who dispatched troops to chase after the suspects, catching them ten *li* [about 5 kilometers or 3.3 miles] west of Guixi. When the criminals arrived at the prison, all confessed as soon as they were interrogated. The prefectural official asked for instructions from the court. The servant who was primarily responsible for the plan was sentenced to death. Lianfu was exiled and died before the order to send him away was issued.

From the beginning to the end, this matter lasted for three years. Bangrong died in the year of *xinhai* in the Shaoxing reign period [1131], Banghua in *renzi* [1132], and Lianfu in *guichou* [1133]. All perished on the eighth day of the sixth month. One could say this is strange.

There is no doubt that arsenic is poisonous, but those who take it do not necessarily all die from it. The calamities of the Wenrens were caused by their evil karma! Those who have unfortunately ingested arsenic and are on the brink of death only need to drink some uncooked oil to induce vomiting. This way, the poison will be gone and do no harm to the body. (*YJZ, bu*:5.1592–93)

95 • Ginger Seller from Huzhou

A petty traveling merchant from Huzhou [in Zhejiang] was selling ginger in Yongjia [in Zhejiang]. Before a mutually agreed-upon price was settled, Wang Sheng, a wealthy man, forcibly put some ginger on the scale. The peddler subsequently uttered some offensive words to Wang. Angered, Wang hit the merchant on the back, and the man fell on the threshold and died. Wang Sheng was extremely terrified. He prayed and tried to resuscitate the merchant, who came back to life a long while later. Wang Sheng wined and dined with the merchant and apologized for his earlier offence. He also fetched a bolt of silk to give to the merchant [as a token of regret].

When the merchant arrived at the ferry crossing on his return trip, the boatman asked where the merchant had gotten the silk. The merchant related to the boatman in detail what had happened and said, "If I had not come back to life after that fall, I would be a ghost in a far-away place!"

At the time, there happened to be a floating corpse within a few miles of the waterway that nobody had claimed. The boatman subsequently had an idea. He bought the silk as well as the bamboo basket from the traveling merchant. After the merchant left, the boatman fetched the floating corpse and transported it to his residence. After taking off his shirt and trousers to clothe the corpse, he ran to knock on Wang Sheng's door and said in a panic, "A guest from Huzhou took the ferry this afternoon. He said that you had almost beat him to death earlier. He also mentioned that he had parents, a wife, and children at home. He entreated that I bring the matter to the authorities and call for his family to remedy the injustice. He left the silk and the basket for me as proof and died soon after. Here is the silk. I thought I should bring this to you and tell you what had happened."

Wang Sheng was shocked to hear the news and became extremely frightened. The whole family cried and implored the boatman, bribing him with two hundred strings of cash coins [for him not to notify the authorities]. Pretending to act against his will, the boatman accepted their pleas reluctantly. Together, they buried the corpse in the deep woods and the boatman moved the next day. No one knew where he had gone.

A sneaky servant at the Wangs learned about this cover-up and extorted Wang repeatedly. Wang was getting tired of the servant, but the blackmailer would not stop. To one's surprise, the servant actually went to the county government to sue Wang Sheng. Wang was thrown in prison. Unable to endure the torture, he died from illness.

The next year, the ginger seller returned and went to visit Wang Sheng's home. Thinking he was a ghost, Wang's family cursed, "Previously, you fell by accident and died. Yet you came back to life later, but you caused our master to die an unnatural death. Have you now come to haunt us?" The guest bowed and sighed in wonder, "I almost died last year and was brought back to life by your family. I am grateful for the silk you gave me. I sold the silk to the boatman and went straight home. I have prepared some local produce to pay back your great kindness. Why do you think I have died and become a ghost?"

[Upon hearing this,] Wang Sheng's son grieved deeply. He asked the merchant to stay at his house, then took the former servant to the government office to have the injustice corrected. Men from the government office also searched for and found and arrested the boatman in a deep valley in Tiantai [in Zhejiang]. Both he and the blackmailing servant died in prison. *This story was told by Wu Zinan.* (*YJZ, bu*:5.1595–96)

96 • Xu Huizhong

Xu Huizhong of Yongjia [in Zhejiang] went to Danyang [in Jiangsu], where he visited a wealthy broker, from whom he borrowed one thousand strings of cash coins. Before Xu paid back the loan, however, the agent died. Because he did not sign a contract when he took the loan, Xu did not tell the agent's family about his debt before he returned home.

Xu later had a son, who was extremely handsome and intelligent. The boy fell ill when he was eight. His parents were worried. The funds they spent on hiring doctors and buying medicines was innumerable. One day, the sick boy suddenly told Wenshi, a nun he was close to, "I now wish to go home." The nun thought the boy's words strange, asking, "Your parents love you so much. Why are you talking about going home?" The boy said, "I was a native of Danyang. Previously, Mr. Xu [the boy's father] borrowed a million cash coins from me, but did not pay it back because I passed away. I have come to fetch it myself. Now that the amount has all been paid for, it is time for me to leave." He died after saying this. *The granddaughter of Huizhong related this to the daughter-in-law of Zhu Hengfu. (YJZ, bu:6.1606)*

97 • Bathhouse in the Capital

In the early years of the Xuanhe reign period [1119–1125], an official waiting for appointment was scheduled to present his credentials in the Department of Personnel. He got up way too early. There were few pedestrians on the road and the gate to the Department was not yet open. He therefore decided to take a short rest at a teahouse.

Inside the teahouse was a bathhouse, which employed a few male servants. Seeing that the official came at such an odd time, the servants thought he must have been a rustic person on his first visit to the capital. It was winter at the time. The guest had on a brown fur coat and was plump, [giving the impression that he was a rich man]. The bathhouse attendants therefore schemed to plot against the official. They stealthily drew a leather noose to tie around his neck, dragged him behind the screen, and threw him onto the ground. By then, the official was near death. The villains, pointing at him, boasted, "Not including the value of the clothes, the meat on this body alone is worth a large amount of money."

Because it was quite some time before dawn, the robbers did not kill the official immediately. A short while later, when the leather ligature had loosened slightly, the official suddenly came back to life. He wished to escape but was afraid he would get lost. While hesitating, he suddenly heard the messengers of the prefect. The official quickly ran out while shouting, "homicide, homicide." The villains were taken by surprise and became extremely nervous, but pretended to stay calm, saying, "Do you have epilepsy?" When the prefect arrived momentarily, the official appealed to him in front of the prefect's horse. The prefect immediately ordered the crooks' arrest. He also had the floors of the bathhouse taken apart, where three bodies were found. The bodies were not even cold yet because the three people had been murdered the previous night. The prefect then had the shop owner's whole family seized and put into prison. The human meat that the shop had minced to sell had all been purchased by young ruffians. *This story was told by Xuangong.* (*YJZ, bu*:8.1625–26)

98 • Hua Buru

Lin Cong of Caozhou [in Shandong] (courtesy name Shenli) once studied at the Imperial University. While napping one day, Lin dreamt about a beautiful woman telling him, "I am the daughter of Legal Researcher Meng in the Western Capital [Luoyang, Henan]. My childhood name is Hua Buru [literally, flowers are not on par with her looks]. When you earn the examination degree in the future, you will serve in Luoyang. Please do not betroth yourself to anyone else." Lin woke up and remembered his dream. Upon telling it to his classmates, all laughed at its absurdity.

Lin earned the examination degree in the third year of the Daguan reign period [1109] and, surely, he was appointed the District Defender of Henan County [Luoyang, Henan]. One day when he went to the Tiannü Temple on business, he got to talk to the old nun there. Lin asked her, "Is there a Legal Researcher Meng here?" The nun said, "There is." "Does he have a daughter?" "Yes. Her name is Hua Buru. She has recently married someone." Lin was shocked [by the accuracy of his dream] and silently suffered the regret of having come too late [for him to marry the girl in his dream].

In her husband's home, Hua Buru also dreamt about a man telling her, "I am Judicial Control Officer Lin. What happened to your agreement to marry me?" When she woke up, Hua Buru secretly searched for and obtained Lin's name, but she did not understand the meaning of "marriage agreement" and certainly did not know that Lin himself had also had a dream.

Only several days after this incident, Hua Buru's husband died. [Upon receiving the news,] Lin immediately sent a matchmaker to negotiate a marriage contract. The agreement was that the two would marry when Hua Buru finished mourning her husband. One day after they were already married, each told the other about their dream. Both were shocked by what had happened for no reason. Three years after the woman married Lin, her former husband returned to haunt her and she subsequently died. Lin later served as the Doctor of the School for the Imperial Family. Every time he told people this story, he could not stop feeling sorrowful. (*YJZ, bu*:10.1636–37)

99 • Predestined Limits on Landowning

The carpenter Wang Jun at Rui'an County in Wenzhou [in Zhejiang] learned his craft at a young age. His work was exquisite, as if it was completed by a person with many years of experience. When he was about seventeen or eighteen, he dreamt of entering a government office, where he saw a clerk passing by holding official documents. Wang Jun asked what those papers were. The clerk answered, "These are the registry of the fortune and life span of those under my jurisdiction." Wang then asked about the prefectures and the townships that the clerk was responsible for; Rui'an was one of them. Jun bowed and entreated the clerk time and again, wanting to know what future he would enjoy. The clerk looked it up and showed the register to him; it said, "Land will not exceed sixty *mu* [ten acres] and life span not over eighty." At the time, Jun already had thirty *mu* of land. He thought, with his skill being so ingenious, if he enjoyed a superior life span, how could he not be rich? For this reason, he did not consider the dream accurate.

Several years later, Wang's landholding reached sixty *mu*. He was also designated a chief craftsman, so his income was substantial, but every time he earned some money, something always came up, and he would spend the income right away. This went on for forty to fifty years. His property actually did not increase. Only then did he understand what the deity had told him years ago. He then stopped managing his properties. Wang Jun died at the age of seventy-nine. *Zhu Huansou of Wenzhou told this story.* (*YJZ, bu*:10.1639–40)

100 • Willing to Die for Mother

Ke Congshi lived in Qingyuan, a village north of Wenzhou [in Zhejiang]. During the Jianyan years [1127–1130], large groups of bandits rose in abundance. They would slaughter whoever they encountered. Residents of Qingyuan all fled to Mount Meng. Before long, the bandits came and killed many villagers; those who were not slaughtered were captured, beaten, and interrogated for the locations where people had hidden their treasures. Congshi's mother was among those caught.

Congshi grieved deeply about his mother's capture and could not bear the thought of his mother dying at the hands of the bandits. He therefore went to the bandits' hideout. Performing a deep bow, he said, "I am the only one who can find the treasures hidden by my fellow villagers. My mother does not know anything. I am willing to substitute myself for my mother and help you find the treasures." The bandits then released Congshi's mother and held him in her place. Congshi led the bandits to several places, but they did not find anything. Only then did the bandits realize that Congshi had been fooling them. [Angered that Congshi had tricked them,] the bandits shot arrows at him, but not one would hit Congshi's body. [Curious about what had happened,] the bandits asked Congshi why he deceived them. Congshi replied that he was afraid that his mother would die an unnatural death. He therefore designed this scheme to die in his mother's place. Moved by Congshi's filial piety, the bandits released him. (*YJZ, sanbu*:1805)

Suggested Reading

Bodde, Dirk. "Some Chinese Tales of the Supernatural." *Harvard Journal of Asiatic Studies* 6, nos. 3–4 (1942): 338–57.

Boltz, Judith. "Not by the Seal of Office Alone: New Weapons in Battles with the Supernatural." In *Religion and Society in T'ang and Sung China*, edited by Patricia Ebrey and Peter Gregory, 241–305. Honolulu: University of Hawaii Press, 1993.

Bossler, Beverly. *Courtesans, Concubines, and the Cult of Female Fidelity*. Cambridge, MA: Harvard University Asia Center, 2013.

Campany, Robert Ford. "Ghosts Matter: The Culture of Ghosts in Six Dynasties *Zhiguai.*" *Chinese Literature: Essays, Articles, Reviews* 13 (December 1991): 15–34.

———. "Return-from-Death Narratives in Early Medieval China." *Journal of Chinese Religions* 18 (1990): 91–125.

———. *Signs from the Unseen Realm: Buddhist Miracle Tales from Medieval China*. Honolulu: University of Hawaii Press, 2012.

———. *Strange Writing: Anomaly Accounts in Early Medieval China*. Albany: State University of New York Press, 1996.

———. *To Live as Long as Heaven and Earth: A Translation and Study of Ge Hong's Traditions of Divine Transcendents*. Berkeley: University of California Press, 2002.

Chaffee, John W. *The Thorny Gates of Learning in Sung China: A Social History of Examinations*. Cambridge: Cambridge University Press, 1985.

Chaffee, John W., and Denis Twitchett, eds. *Cambridge History of China*. Vol. 5, pt. 2, *Sung China, 960–1279*. Cambridge: Cambridge University Press, 2015.

Chan, Tak-hung. *The Discourse on Foxes and Ghosts: Ji Yun and Eighteenth-Century Literati Storytelling*. Honolulu: University of Hawaii Press, 1998.

Chang Fu-jui. "Hong Hao, Hong Kua, and Hong Mai." In *Sung Biographies*, edited by Herbert Franke, 464–78. Wiesbaden: Steiner, 1976.

Chen, Kenneth. "Filial Piety in Chinese Buddhism." *Harvard Journal of Asiatic Studies* 28 (1968): 81–97.

Cherniack, Susan. "Book Culture and Textual Transmission in Sung China." *Harvard Journal of Asiatic Studies* 54, no. I (June 1994): 5–125.

Chia, Lucille. *Printing for Profit: The Commercial Publishers of Jianyang, Fujian (11th–17th Centuries)*. Cambridge, MA: Harvard University Asia Center, 2002.

Clark, Hugh R. *Portrait of a Community: Society, Culture, and the Structures of Kinship in the Mulan River Valley (Fujian) from the Late Tang through the Song*. Hong Kong: Chinese University Press, 2007.

Cohen, Alvin P. "Avenging Ghosts and Moral Judgment in Ancient Chinese Historiography: Three Examples from *Shih-chi*." In *Legend, Lore, and Religion in China: Essays in Honor of Wolfram Eberhard on His Seventieth Birthday*, edited by Alvin P. Cohen and Sarah Allan, 97–108. San Francisco: Chinese Materials Center, 1979.

———. *Tales of Vengeful Souls: A Sixth Century Collection of Chinese Avenging Ghost Stories*. Variétés sinologiques, n.s., 68. Paris: Institut Ricci, Centre d'études chinoises, 1982.

Cole, Alan. *Mothers and Sons in Chinese Buddhism*. Stanford, CA: Stanford University Press, 1998.

Davis, Edward L. *Society and the Supernatural in Song China*. Honolulu: University of Hawaii Press, 2001.

Dudbridge, Glen. *Religious Experience and Lay Society in T'ang China: A Reading of Tai Fu's Kuang-i chi*. Cambridge: Cambridge University Press, 1995.

———. *The Tale of Li Wa: Study and Critical Edition of a Chinese Story from the Ninth Century*. London: Ithaca Press for the Board of the Faculty of Oriental Studies, Oxford University, 1983.

Ebrey, Patricia. "Concubines in Sung China." *Journal of Family History* 11 (1986): 1–24.

———. "Cremation in Sung China." *American Historical Review* 95 (1990): 406–28.

———. *The Inner Quarters: Marriage and the Lives of Chinese Women in the Sung Period*. Berkeley: University of California Press, 1993.

———. "Sung Neo-Confucian Views on Geomancy." In *Meeting of Minds: Festschrift for W. T. Chan and Wm. T. de Bary*, edited by Irene Bloom and Joshua A. Fogel, 75–107. New York: Columbia University Press, 1997.

Ebrey, Patricia, and Peter Gregory, eds. *Religion and Society in T'ang and Sung China*. Honolulu: University of Hawaii Press, 1993.

Egan, Ronald. "On the Circulation of Books during the Eleventh and Twelfth Centuries." *Chinese Literature: Essays, Articles, Reviews* 30 (December 2008): 9–17.

Franke, Herbert, ed. *The Cambridge History of China.* Vol. 6, *Alien Regimes and Border States, 907–1368.* Cambridge: Cambridge University Press, 1994.

Fu Daiwie. "A Contextual and Taxonomic Study of the 'Divine Marvels' and 'Strange Occurrences' in the *Mengxi bitan.*" *Chinese Science* 11 (1993–1994): 3–35.

Gardner, Daniel. "Ghosts and Spirits in the Sung Neo-Confucian World: Chu Hsi on kuei-shen." *Journal of the American Oriental Society* 115, no. 4 (1995): 598–611.

Hansen, Valerie. *Changing Gods in Medieval China, 1127–1276.* Princeton, NJ: Princeton University Press, 1990.

———. *Negotiating Daily Life in Traditional China: How Ordinary People Used Contracts, 600–1400.* New Haven, CT: Yale University Press, 1995.

Hymes, Robert. "Gossip as History: Hong Mai's *Yijian zhi* and the Place of Oral Anecdotes in Song Historical Knowledge." *Chūgoku shigaku* 21 (2011): 1–28.

———. *Way and Byway: Taoism, Local Religion, and Models of Divinity in Sung and Modern China.* Berkeley: University of California Press, 2002.

Inglis, Alister. "Hong Mai's Informants for the *Yijian zhi.*" *Journal of Song-Yuan Studies* 32 (2002): 83–125.

———. *Hong Mai's Record of the Listener and Its Song Dynasty Context.* Albany: State University of New York Press, 2006.

———. "A Textual History of Hong Mai's *Yijian zhi.*" *T'oung Pao* 93, nos. 4–5 (2007): 283–368.

Johnson, David. "The City-God Cults of T'ang and Sung China." *Harvard Journal of Asiatic Studies* 45, no. 2 (December 1985): 363–457.

Kuhn, Dieter. *The Age of Confucian Rule: The Song Transformation of China.* Cambridge, MA: Belknap Press, 2009.

Lagerwey, John. *Taoist Ritual in Chinese Society and History.* New York: Macmillan, 1987.

Lee, Thomas H. C. *Government Education and Examinations in Sung China.* Hong Kong: Chinese University Press, 1985.

Liao Hsien-huei. "Encountering Evil: Ghosts and Demonic Forces in the Lives of the Song Elite." *Journal of Song-Yuan Studies* 37 (2007): 89–134.

———. "Experiencing the 'Lesser Arts': The Mantic Arts and Experts in the Lives of Song Literati." *New History* 20, no. 4 (2009): 1–58.

———. "Exploring Weal and Woe: The Song Elite's Mantic Beliefs and Practices." *T'oung Pao* 91, nos. 4–5 (2005): 347–95.

———. "Geomancy and Burial: The Social Status of the Song Geomancers." *Studies in Urban Cultures* 10 (2008): 96–115.

————. "Praying for a Revelation: The Mental Universe of the Song Examination Candidates." *New History* 15, no. 4 (2004): 41–92.

————. "Visualizing the Afterlife: The Song Elite's Obsession with Death, the Underworld, and Salvation." *Chinese Studies* 20, no. 1 (2002): 399–440.

Lo, Winston W. *An Introduction to the Civil Service of Sung China: With Emphasis on Its Personnel Administration.* Honolulu: University of Hawaii Press, 1987.

Lorge, Peter. *The Reunification of China: Peace through War under the Song Dynasty.* Cambridge: Cambridge University Press, 2015.

McKnight, Brian E. *Law and Order in Sung China.* Cambridge: Cambridge University Press, 1992.

————. *Village and Bureaucracy in Southern Sung China.* Chicago: University of Chicago Press, 1971.

Mollier, Christine. *Buddhism and Taoism Face to Face: Scripture, Ritual, and Iconographic Exchange in Medieval China.* Honolulu: University of Hawaii Press, 2009.

Strickmann, Michel. *Chinese Magical Medicine.* Edited by Bernard Faure. Stanford, CA: Stanford University Press, 2001.

Teiser, Stephen F. *The Ghost Festival in Medieval China.* Princeton, NJ: Princeton University Press, 1988.

Ter Haar, Barend. "Newly Recovered Anecdotes from Hong Mai's (1123–1202) *Yijian zhi.*" *Journal of Song-Yuan Studies* 23 (1993): 19–41.

————. *Telling Stories: Witchcraft and Scapegoating in Chinese History.* Leiden: Brill, 2006.

Twitchett, Denis, and Paul Jakov Smith, eds. *The Cambridge History of China.* Vol. 5, pt. 1, *The Sung Dynasty and Its Precursors, 907–1279.* Cambridge: Cambridge University Press, 2009.

Von Glahn, Richard. *Fountain of Fortune: Money and Monetary Policy in China, 1000–1700.* Berkeley: University of California Press, 1996.

Xu, Man. *Crossing the Gate: Everyday Lives of Women in Song Fujian (960–1279).* Albany: State University of New York Press, 2016.

Yu, Anthony C. "'Rest, Rest, Perturbed Spirit!' Ghosts in Traditional Chinese Prose Fiction." *Harvard Journal of Asiatic Studies* 47, no. 2 (December 1987): 397–434.

Zhang, Cong Ellen. "Anecdotal Writing on Illicit Sex in Song China (960–1279)." *Journal of the History of Sexuality* 22, no. 2 (2013): 255–82.

————. "Negative Role Models: Unfilial Stories in Song *Biji* (Miscellaneous Writing)." In *Behaving Badly in Early and Medieval China,* edited by N.

Harry Rothschild and Leslie V. Wallace, 39–55. Honolulu: University of Hawaii Press, 2017.

————. "Of Revelers and Witty Conversationalists: Song (960–1279) *Biji* Writing and the Rise of a New Literati Ideal." *Chinese Historical Review* 23, no. 2 (2016): 130–46.

————. "Things Heard in the Past, Material for Future Use: A Study of Song (960–1279) *biji* Prefaces." *East Asian Publishing and Society* 6, no. 1 (2016): 22–53.

————. "To Be 'Erudite in Miscellaneous Knowledge': A Study of Song (960–1279) *Biji* Writing." *Asia Major*, 3rd ser., 25, no. 2 (2012): 43–77.

————. *Transformative Journeys: Travel and Culture in Song (960–1279) China.* Honolulu: University of Hawaii Press, 2011.

Thematic Guide to the 100 Stories

Natural, Political, and Social and Economic Conditions

Crime and punishment: 8, 23, 24, 26, 39, 44, 51, 56, 58, 66, 71, 72, 75, 80, 86, 94, 95, 97

Jin conquest and rule of north China: 20, 29, 50, 61, 62, 71, 73, 100

Local Businesses: 2, 26, 32, 43, 76, 94, 96, 97. *See also* Travel, Inns

Local government: 1, 8, 9, 19, 20, 21, 23, 24, 33, 39, 47, 49, 51, 53, 58, 91, 94, 95

Market: 25, 26, 36, 47, 56, 65, 71, 92

Natural disasters: 52, 60, 62, 63, 79

Travel: 8, 23, 28, 31, 40, 41, 45, 61, 66, 78, 80, 87, 95

    Inns: 19, 23, 40, 58, 66, 87

Beliefs and Practices

Animals: 11, 23, 31, 47, 66, 82, 83, 84, 92

Buddhist temples: 3, 6, 10, 18, 20, 28, 74, 78, 80, 83

Cremation: 27, 28, 45

Divination, fortune-telling, and geomancy: 2, 14, 21, 22, 30, 40, 50, 63, 70, 77, 81, 87, 99

Dreams: 1, 12, 13, 18, 22, 28, 39, 40, 44, 45, 46, 48, 49, 55, 57, 65, 74, 82, 83, 90, 98, 99

Ghosts: 5, 7, 8, 28, 33, 34, 38, 41, 43, 50, 54, 69, 75, 86, 87, 89

Heaven, gods, and spirits: 3, 15, 18, 23, 25, 40, 42, 46, 51, 52, 53, 62, 63, 68

Hell or underworlds: 10, 12, 22, 36, 39, 60, 67, 72, 74, 85, 99

Karma, retribution: 19, 25, 27, 29, 34, 40, 52, 53, 67, 74, 82, 83, 91, 92, 94, 96

Local deities, beliefs, and practices: 1, 12, 13, 24, 49, 62, 63, 65

Notions about destiny and fate: 16, 20, 21, 28, 30, 40, 46, 49, 70, 84, 98, 99

Reincarnation and transmigration: 10, 11, 37, 48, 67, 82, 83, 91, 92, 96

Spirit possession and exorcism: 24, 34, 41, 44, 54

Strange beings: 6, 61, 64, 76

People of All Walks of Life

Buddhist monks; 10, 18, 20, 28, 42, 48, 58, 74, 77, 78, 80, 83

Butchers: 11, 71, 82

Daoist masters, ritualists, and exorcists: 2, 4, 14, 32, 34, 38, 54, 56, 77, 81, 88

Diviners, fortune-tellers, and geomancers: *See* Divination, fortune-telling, geomancy

Doctors: 4, 16, 70, 94

  Illness, cures, and prescriptions: 3, 4, 14, 35, 39, 79, 94

Maids and wet nurses: 14, 27, 33, 34, 45

Merchants: 3, 8, 19, 20, 23, 26, 40, 66, 75, 95

Runners and clerks: 9, 24, 47, 51, 69, 84, 91

Scholar-officials: 1, 9, 12, 21, 24, 28, 31, 32, 33, 35, 37, 38, 40, 41, 43, 44, 46, 57, 59, 66, 67, 79, 80, 87, 90, 91, 97, 98

Servants: 11, 37, 43, 73, 76, 95

Students and examination candidates: 4, 12, 13, 19, 20, 22, 28, 31, 37, 40, 50, 61

  Imperial University: 4, 12, 19, 22, 45

Thieves, robbers, and bandits: 8, 17, 20, 23, 26, 50, 64, 66, 72, 73, 93, 97, 100

Marriage and Sexuality

Concubines and courtesans: 6, 34, 38, 55, 69, 75

Female chastity: 17, 93

Illicit sexual conduct and relationships: 4, 28, 33, 40, 51, 52, 58, 61, 71, 74, 80

Marriage and remarriage: 5, 38, 39, 40, 46, 54, 55, 89, 98

Moral conduct (men): 16, 19, 26, 40, 71, 73

Spousal relations/jealousy: 5, 34, 54, 55, 80

Family Relationships and Family Matters

Debt and property-related matters: 10, 11, 15, 23, 29, 48, 49, 75, 85, 86, 94, 95, 96, 99

Family life and family relationships: 2, 6, 14, 31, 32, 33, 36, 42, 49, 53, 55, 56, 59, 68, 81, 82, 85, 86, 87, 89, 93, 94, 96

(Un)Filial piety

  Unfiliality: 12, 13, 15, 22, 25, 42, 50, 52, 53, 68, 82, 92

  Filial piety: 31, 56, 59, 67, 71, 83, 90, 91, 100

Tombs and burial-related matters: 12, 13, 22, 24, 28, 30, 38, 41, 45, 49, 60, 64, 77, 81, 83, 87, 90